Stephen Land

With K.C. Wells

Copyright notice

Dedication

"The Race" is dedicated to all of the children, teens and adults that have been affected by sexual abuse and or bullying. Most assume that suicide is the best way to make a statement but in all honesty it's not. Speaking out and sharing your story is the only true way to bring change, awareness, and healing to ourselves and others.

I dedicate my story for the encouragement of others to share their stories. I dedicate my life to advocate for those who cannot speak for themselves, and to be an activist on behalf of the issues of sexual assault and bullying.

I dedicate this book to those who have lost their lives because of the effects of sexual abuse and bullying. May you rest in peace.

A percentage of proceeds from "The Race" and "The Race to Self-Identity" series will be donated to 1in6.org.

The Race

Prologue

Some realizations are tough. Take it from me.

My name is Stephen Land, it is the summer of 2015 and I am struggling. I have all of this built up emotion that has not yet been dealt with and I don't know where to start. I've done counseling. I've prayed. Some days are great; some weeks are great, some months and even some years. Maybe I am just putting my fears and emotions into boxes and they are getting too full. Full to over flowing, in fact.

Maybe it's time for me to start really *dealing with some of these things.*

Sometimes you are put into situations where you are forced to do things, experience things, feel things: things that used to trigger; things that you thought you could handle.

It has been over a year since I stopped going to therapy and I find myself struggling in some situations. I hyperventilate to the point where I cannot breathe. I have high anxiety. Sometimes depression kicks in and I fall.

I try never to fall so far that I cannot get back up. I try to maintain a support network; this is key to keeping me from getting to that point. I have had boyfriends, partners that I could only dream of having. Sometimes they seems too good to be true, but they challenged me. Challenged me to be myself, to

not be afraid and to be strong in tough situations. Challenged my emotions and my abilities in a way that no one else really can. It is a tough thing to say but here goes: I am far from being truly healed from my past but I am truly better than I have been.

Some days are good, some weeks are good, some months are good, but there are some things that trigger things locked in the deepest depths of my heart and I fall. I overthink things. I cry and I run, straight into walls that block me from getting over. I look for comfort but instead all I find is my memories giving me a solid slap in the face.

There have been times when I thought I was there, finally over it all and finally at a point where I could stand on my own two feet again. But then something triggers and I lose control, I go crazy and have no physical or mental ability to stop it.

Sometimes I hold on tight to things or people because I am afraid of losing them, afraid that if I let go, I would be left to face this world—my past—all alone. I was strong at one point but right now? I am at a low ebb, confronted by the tough realization that I need to go to therapy again. I need to go even when I feel strong, and go until I know for sure I can stand without falling.

I don't want to be crazy.

I don't want to overthink.

I don't want to fall any more.

I want to be free of the entire emotional and mental struggle.

I want to have peace in my heart and I want most of all to be strong again.
This is my story.

Day One - Fuck Lemons

When life gives you lemons, you squeeze the hell out of them until you no longer have the ability to squeeze.

Obviously, I have some things to work out but this *truth*, this is how I have been feeling lately, and yeah, it's not been good. I have nothing left to lose, especially when it seems like nothing good can come out of this world. Life seems to be a relentless conveyor belt, dishing up hurt after hurt, pain after pain—and no one else cares! *No one* is going to just hand over an opportunity for no reason. This world doesn't give *two shits* about who you are, who you know, or whose dick you suck. If you want something, you have to take it.

Sadly for me, everyone else figured this out before I did and they took *everything* from me.

My dignity—gone. Taken.

My childhood—gone. Taken.

My ability to trust.

My virginity.

My hopes.

My dreams...

Yeah, you get the picture, right?

Somehow, by some miracle, I have been able to maintain my ability to love, although it seems as if others haven't found the ability to love me back in

9

quite the same way. Like I said before, hurt after hurt and pain after pain, it's the story of my life. It seems like no matter where I go, no matter how far I move from where the pain started, I can't get away from it. I cannot run fast enough or far enough.

Life catches up. It finds me and plunges me back into the deep darkness, and there I am, back into this very spot over and over again.

Fuck lemons!

By now I'm sure you are wondering; *what is this guy talking about? Why is he bursting at the seams with self-pity? And what part of life keeps catching up to him?*

Hold on to your seats because it's going to be a bumpy ride.

Today is April 11, 2015.

My name is Stephen. I am just this ordinary guy with an ordinary name. I'm in the hospital, but lucky me, this is the day I get to go home. I have spent the last five days being pricked, prodded and poked every four hours to do blood work, woken up at four a.m. to be weighed, and served the worst food *ever* produced by 'certified chefs.' Although that all sounds pretty daunting, that wasn't the worst part about having to spend five nights in the hospital.

I had over *one hundred forty-four hours* to do nothing but think, think some more, and over think. Oh yeah, and I also got to remember—maybe it was more a case that I was *forced* to remember—and it terrified the shit out of me.

I can hear you from here: *Remember what?*

Well, since I had pen and paper handy I can share those memories with you.

Day One – Admitted

It was April 6, 2015
9:00 AM
It all started when I walked into the emergency room. After checking in, I sat in the waiting room. I am not even sure how I even made it here, because my pain was so close to boiling point I felt like I was going to explode.

That's where the recollections began. There was a commercial on the waiting room TV about a show called "American Crime." This show had a series coming up that would feature a boy who'd been sexually assaulted and would focus on rape culture, and how it affects boys as well as girls.

My mind was rolling all over the place. I was holding back tears because that boy was me.

A boy living in a straight, conservative world. Afraid.

No, not afraid—*terrified*—of what others might think if they learned he'd been sexually abused.

But that's not even where it ended. The boy was also gay, closeted and living in a community where such a lifestyle wasn't accepted.

This was my story too.

Okay, so it wasn't *really* my story but in a way it was.

Confused? Join the club.

I was sitting there, fighting through the pain, through whatever was happening in my body that had brought me to the hospital in the first place, and trying to control my emotions.

I was at an all-time low.

10:00 AM

Finally the little receptionist lady who sat at the front desk called out my name.

Okay, so she yelled 'Ste-f-on" and that *not* being my name, I didn't react, but then she yelled *Mr. Land.* I wobbled in pain to the front desk, and they took me to a small room where they took my blood pressure and weight, then asked me a million questions about why I'd come into the hospital. I bore it for as long as I could, and then I opened my eyes wide.

"All you need to know is that I am in a *lot of pain* here, and I need to know the hell why!"

The nurse grabbed a light, took a closer look at my eyes and suddenly everything changed. They rushed me into my own room, while she mumbled to the other nurses that I had jaundice.

Now, I grew up in Phoenix, Arizona, where I hung out with all the black girls. To me, Jaundice sounded like a name of a girl I went to school with. Pain or not, I couldn't help my reaction. I began to giggle.

The nurse took one look at me and called out that I was becoming hysterical.

No one ever called me funny before. I was in so much pain that I wasn't really making any sense of what was happening. I was giggling, crying, and still thinking about Jaundice.

The room was empty for what seemed like five or ten minutes until a little old woman walked in. Her English was terrible but she was so incredibly sweet. She attached a needle to my vein and hooked me up to an IV bag, then she took four vials of blood and pumped me full of morphine. With that, she turned on the TV and walked out of the room.

This was my first experience on morphine, and I was high as a kite. The HGTV home and garden channel was on, and the Property Brothers were in the middle of demolition when I passed out.

I woke up to two big dudes turning off the TV before they wheeled me out into the hallway. I was confused as to what was going on. Once in the hallway the morphine again took over and I passed out.

12:30 PM

The morphine was no longer working and I was in tears again. I sent a text to my then partner David who was on his lunch break. His response? '*Yell at the nurses and demand medication.*' A passing nurse noticed my tears and reacted instantly with another dose of morphine, but this time a stronger dose. Thankfully it went to work fast. I didn't pass out this time, but faded in and out of sleep, periodically sending texts to David to reassure him I was doing

okay.

4:00PM

David was off work and sitting next to me in the hallway of the emergency room. We were up against the wall, close enough to the nurses' station that we could hear the phones ringing and the nurses' inappropriate work chatter. Unfortunately, we were far enough away that they couldn't see us or hear us when we called. Since I was in the hallway I didn't have a call button to request assistance if I needed medication or to use the restroom. The important thing was, David was there with me and I was comfortable enough to go to sleep.

5:30 PM

The morphine started to wear off.

6.00 PM

I was in pain, crying and squeezing David's hand like I was about to die. The nurse came over to ask if I was okay—clearly I wasn't—and then she walked away when I told her I needed something for the pain.

7:00 PM

The nurse finally returned, but only to tell me the doctor would be there to see me in ten minutes' time.

At last!

8:30 PM

There was still no doctor, I was still sitting in the hallway, still crying, still in extreme pain, and David was pissed.

That was when things got ugly.

David asked for a doctor and demanded I receive something for the pain. The nurse started yelling at him, telling him she had patients that were a higher priority than me. Through my haze of pain, I recalled not having even seen this nurse before. Then *she* got pissed and called security, telling them to escort David from the hospital.

Pain or not, I had had enough. I demanded that if security removed David, they also remove me. And if that happened, they'd better damn well hope nothing happened to me, because that would come right back down to her liability and hers alone.

Unsurprisingly, she backed down.

Sensible woman.

9:00 PM

Five minutes after the blow up, the doctor was finally at my bedside. By then the pain was so severe, my body had begun to go numb. I could no longer feel my feet or hands, except for the odd tingle that shot through my legs.

I was deteriorating.

According to David, the blood vessels in my face started popping and my eyes became bloodshot, covered with a jaundiced film that had only gotten worse since my arrival in the hospital. Come to think of it, *everything* had gotten worse since that point.

10:00 PM

I was finally in a room on the sixth floor, my roommate an older gentleman who was happy to see

someone who could actually carry out a conversation and who wasn't going senile.

And *at last*, there were results from the blood work. My liver enzyme levels were at 5,500 and I'd gone into acute liver failure. It seemed I'd consumed something contaminated and had developed Hepatitis A which had attacked my liver, hence all the pain. I had a week in the hospital to look forward to, along with talks with the New York City Department of Health, the CDC and a whole slew of doctors. Not to mention a complete change of diet.

I hated it. My freedom of movement severely curtailed, I felt trapped. The last time I'd been in any situation remotely similar, I'd blacked out a lot and suffered from flashbacks of my childhood.

NOT a place I wanted to be. I didn't want to relive all that shit. The flashbacks always ended up with the same outcome—they pushed me toward depression and intensified my obsessive-compulsive habits. Add to that the fact that I'd never spent the night in a hospital before, and I was feeling decidedly nervous. Thank God David was there. He agreed to visit me before work every morning and as soon as he got off work, until I fell asleep.

Right then, I knew one thing—David loved me.

You're all dying to know how I got in that mess, right? So let's back up a little.

My sickness began with a Mexican dinner.

March 20, 2015

I'd been dancing a few times a month in Queens

for one of the few gay bars that existed outside of Manhattan. After more than seven years of working in nightlife I'd learned pretty quick that I had to eat at least two hours before dancing, so I didn't end up barfing all over the clientele. The management tended to view such behavior in a dim light.

Imagine that.

Go figure.

So, I headed off to enjoy what New Yorkers call a "lovely Mexican meal" with my friend Flo. I enjoyed a Chicken Burrito with rice and no beans. I also treated myself with a strawberry frozen margarita. We finished dinner with about two and a half hours before call time, so I was good to go.

Only this time, my routine didn't work out so well.

A few minutes into my first dance, my stomach began to hurt really badly. Afraid the world was about to fall out of my ass, I ran to the restroom, only when I got there, I threw up everywhere. I couldn't even lay the blame on alcohol, because I'd only had the one drink with dinner. When I got back up to dance, the pain in my stomach started up again, only now it had crept over into my back as well.

Then it struck me. This had to be due to some injury I'd caused myself during my very first kettle bell workout earlier that day. The pain wasn't showing any signs of decreasing, so I called it a night and jumped into a cab to head home. On the way the pain got so bad I decided I wanted to go to the

hospital so I sent a text to David, telling him. When I saw his reply, I was really feeling the love: David told me to stop exaggerating.

So what did I do?

I went home. Bad decision #1.

March 23, 2015

Not only was the pain still with me, I could barely move because of it. My back was that bad, just *breathing* sent pain rippling through it. It was at this point I decided I'd *really* hurt myself badly. Maybe what I needed was some time off from working out my back. Maybe then the pain would go away.

Bad decision #2.

March 30, 2015

I was in so much pain from my back, I was in tears. I didn't have a clue what was happening to me. The boyfriend gave me some Naproxen which did help to ease the pain but I wasn't sure I could carry on like that. When David finally asked me if I wanted to go to the hospital, I refused. I'd spent so much time with my father in hospital that just the smell freaked me out. Of course, in hindsight, I should have listened to David and gone there anyway.

Yeah. Bad decision #3.

April 3, 2015 – April 4, 2015

I was ready to try dancing again. I made it

through all of my sets for both days, but had to take both days off from my day job in order to do so. In those two nights I made five times what I'd have made from the day job.

April 6, 2015

There was pain *everywhere*. Back, stomach, head and all points between. There was pressure to pass a bowel movement, so I crawled from the bed to the bathroom, but nothing materialized. I didn't think I could even make it back to the bed so I crawled from the bathroom to the living room to lie down on the couch in tears. When David appeared, ready for work, he took one look at me and got scared. I had no choice: if things got worse I'd walk to the hospital. It was only two blocks away, for God's sake.

Finally, I was making some sense.

David left for work and I tried to eat, but couldn't even keep down two bites of my cereal. By 9.00 a.m. I grabbed my wallet and headed to the emergency room.

So there you have it. My stupid choices made things worse and in the end I paid the price for it. But hey, at least I made the choice to finally get to the hospital.

Day Two – Flashbacks

April 7, 2015

Morning

I opened my eyes slowly, adjusting to the light. "Wha time is it?" I asked groggily.

"Four a.m. We're just taking blood."

I blinked. A different nurse from the one I'd last seen. Then I blinked again. "What time did you say?" I peered at her intently, her features gradually becoming more distinct.

She flashed me a tight smile. "Better get used to it. We'll be taking blood every four hours. We also need to get you out of bed so we can weigh you."

Weigh me? Now I got it. I was still asleep.

Details began to filter through my still sleep-numbed brain. A plastic pad gripped my finger. A room. I was in a room, and it was much damn quieter than the ER had been, except there was the constant quiet beep of the monitor next to my bed.

One thing hadn't changed, however. I was still in pain.

Before I could say anything about it, two strong arms helped me to sit, before another pair of arms joined them.

"That's it," a new voice said, her tone laced with encouragement. "We've got you." I groaned and they stilled instantly. "Are you in pain?"

"Yes," I whispered, as if speaking any louder would increase it.

"Right, we'll see about that when we're done."

The weighing over, I was helped back into bed. The nurse checked the IV line while the second nurse disappeared from view to return with a vial. It wasn't long before I began to feel the effects of the morphine. God, the *relief*. I sagged into the pillow, that groggy feeling washing over me as the painkillers did their stuff. I followed the conversation between the two nurses, but their words drifted through my fogged brain as I sank deeper into the welcoming arms of pain-free oblivion…

Until something jarred in my head. Something about her little boy…

"Oh my God, what did you say?"

A quiet chuckle. "I didn't want to shout at him. I mean, he's only six, he had no idea what mommy and daddy were doing. I just told him to go back to bed and I'd be in shortly." Another chuckle. "It did sorta ruin the mood though." She sighed. "Oh well. Another time, I guess. Trouble is, times have been few and far between lately."

"Poor little Teddy. You've probably scarred him for life. Kids are really impressionable at that age."

"I'm waiting for the questions, because you just know they're gonna come. Well, he can wait. I am *not* talking about sex to a six-year-old."

"Yeah, let him hold onto his childhood a little

while longer."

Their voices faded as they moved out of range.

I was suddenly wide awake.

A memory had me in its grip and I couldn't free myself. It was so vivid, it was as if I was *there*, back at that party, that hateful day when my life changed forever. No matter what I did, I couldn't turn off the images in my brain. The recollection of odors, sounds, textures. Everything collided and I wanted to cry out, to tell my brain to go fuck itself and *leave me the fuck alone.*

By the time David arrived at that morning, I was a mess.

"Hey, what's wrong?"

His voice broke through and I latched onto it. "Thank God you're here."

He helped me into a sitting position and then sat on the bed beside me. "What's going on, Stephen?"

I was shaking. "Flashbacks." It was all I needed to say. He knew.

"Babe, is there anything I can do?"

Tears rushed down my face as I planted my head on his shoulder. No words were needed.

"Oh hell." His hand curled around mine. There was nothing else he could say.

A few minutes passed and all I could think about was my journals as a kid. I recalled the brief respite I'd gotten from putting everything on paper, how it had helped pull me out of the feelings that had overwhelmed me.

The same feelings I was having now.

It was like my body was telling me to write.

"Babe, I have an idea. Could you do something for me before you leave?"

"Sure."

"Can you go buy me a notepad, or anything you can find to write in?"

David regarded me steadily. "What's the plan?"

I took a deep breath. "I figure if I get everything down on paper, it'll help. Sort of like I'm exorcising a ghost." I snorted. "I have a few of those, right?"

He patted my hand. "I'll go see what I can find." He got up from the bed and kissed my cheek. "I'll be as quick as I can." I knew he didn't have long anyway before he'd have to go to work.

Once he'd left, I lay there, staring at the ceiling. It still felt like it had all happened yesterday. I knew how it was with the flashbacks. It was like being plunged into a pool, the torrents covering my head while I did my best to tread water.

Ten minutes later David was back, a notepad and pen in his hand. "Will these do?"

I gave him a hopefully more positive smile. "That's perfect."

David pulled out his phone and grimaced. "I'm sorry, babe, but I have to go. I'll stop by after work, okay?"

I nodded and accepted his peck on the cheek. I watched him walk out of the door and then I sank back into the pillows.

This is tricky.

I had to find a way to… distance myself from the glut of memories. They still felt too raw, too sharp. Then it came to me.

Pretend it didn't happen to you. Pretend it all happened to someone else. Write it like you're writing about a stranger. Dispassionately. Objectively. Like a reporter or journalist, documenting from the outside.

From a distance.

I opened the notepad and stared at the clean white page. *How the hell do I start this? Where do I start it?*

There was only one answer.

Start at the beginning.

The sun was bright, I remember. It was supposed to be in the upper 90's that day and it was my birthday. I was turning six years old, but who cares, right? Six was just a number, nothing extravagant like five, one, and eighteen or twenty-one. I had ten more years before the next big thing in my life. So what was there to celebrate? Well, life, happiness and the ability to be normal, the fact that I was alive.

I picked up the pen and began to write about Mark. It was easier not to write about myself, so from then on I was Mark.

Day Two - Life Changing Moment

April 22, 1995.

The sun was peaking over the horizon when preparations began for the celebration. Mark, his sister Alyssa and his little brother Lloyd all had their birthdays within nine days of each other, but it was a tradition to celebrate together with one massive birthday. Financially, it made better sense. Just after noon the trickle of friends and family arriving began, soon swelling into a flood, and it wasn't long before the smell of burning charcoal filled the air. It was one of those dry, hot days where after ten minutes outside you were dying of thirst. Only Phoenix tended to be like that most of the year.

The pile of gifts begged to be opened. Mark went last, of course, because he was the eldest: Alyssa had just turned five and Lloyd was four. Mark slowly opened his gifts, careful not to tear the paper to shreds. He received a few pairs of clothes, a box of Lego and some more Hot Wheels. That was great: what was not so good was the absence of one of his best friends from the party. It wasn't as if his missing buddy had needed his parents to give him a ride over—they were neighbors.

Something felt *wrong*.

Mark waited until the party was looking like it was coming to an end, and then asked his mom if he

could go to Javi's house to play when all the guests had gone. Of course she said yes; anything to make him happy on his birthday. Javi was one of the few friends who ever came over to the house. He was one of Mark's three best friends, the other two being Tony and Geo. The four of them were inseparable; they'd sat together in the classroom from kindergarten into first grade. Somehow luck had been with them and they'd all been placed with the same teacher. They hung together during recess and lunch, when they'd chase girls and act the fool without getting into too much trouble.

Mark rang the doorbell. Javi's father, Mr. S appeared.

"Hey, it's the birthday boy!" He let Mark in and led him to Javi's room. Javi was sitting on his bed, looking miserable.

"Why didn't you come over today?" Mark demanded, the words tumbling out of him before Javi had the chance to open his mouth. It still hurt that his friend had missed the party.

Javi let out a heavy sigh. "Dad wouldn't let me leave because I had chores and yard work to do before I could do anything else or go anyplace."

"Did you get it all done?" When Javi nodded, Mark grinned. "Well, then, what are we gonna do?" Javi reached under the bed for the crate that contained all his Lego pieces, and the two boys spent the next hour playing.

"Boys! Come here, please," Mr. S yelled out

from the other room. Mark and Javi left their creations and went into the room where Mr. S worked when he was at home. They stood by his desk and he swiveled round in his chair to look at them. "Boys, you ever played house before?"

The question immediately struck Mark as curious. He hesitated to answer, his cheeks burning, because when they played house, he'd always wanted to play the mom or the caretaker, while Javi was always the dad.

"'*Course* we have, Dad! That's all the girls at school ever want to play," Javi blurted out. Mark was secretly relieved for the save, thankful not to have to reveal anything.

"Well, we're going to play the adult version of house today, boys. I think you're old enough to understand it now." His words made Mark's chest swell with pride. After all, he was six years old now.

Mr. S led them to a room at the back of the house, which took three different keys to open it, much to Mark's surprise. Inside, it was dark and cold, and for the first time, Mark shivered. In the center of the room, against the back wall was a bed, a nightstand on each side, the bed illuminated by a single dim lamp. The closet had no door, just a few boxes piled up inside it with the word Media written on their sides. There was no natural light: the windows were all boarded up and covered with a black fabric.

The room felt like a dungeon, so different from

the rest of the house that was full of color.

Mark's heart pounded when Mr. S opened the nightstand and pulled out a gun. He placed it carefully on the nightstand and regarded them, his expression impassive.

"Now boys, no one is *ever* to know about what we're doing here today, you got that? Because if you ever tell *anyone*...." He picked up the gun and examined it, running his finger along the barrel, before pointing it at the two boys. "Then you two will be dead." Then the gun was placed back on the nightstand, its barrel still pointing in their direction. "Now I'm gonna leave this here, so you don't forget what I just said, okay?"

As if Mark was *ever* going to forget those chilling words or the sight of that gun.

"You're gonna keep quiet now and do what I tell you, is that clear?"

His legs shaking, Mark nodded, his head bobbing rapidly. Out of the corner of his eye, he could see Javi beside him, doing the same.

Mr. S sat down heavily on the bed and regarded them. "Take each other's clothes off."

Puzzled but too scared to say anything, Mark helped Javi with his shirt, then his basketball shorts. Javi did the same for Mark. When they'd gotten down to their socks and underwear, they stood in front of Mr. S. He gestured toward them. "And the rest." In silence the two boys removed the remaining garments while Mr. S nodded in approval.

"Mark, get down on your knees in front of Javi."

Mark complied, wondering where this was going. Then Mr. S's tone changed. "Suck on Javi's penis, like a good boy?" His tone reminded Mark of his little sister in the candy store, begging their mom for something. But that was pushed out of his mind when Mr. S placed his hand on the gun and pointed it directly at Mark. "Do it, or do I have to remind you of what will happen?"

Tears welled up in Mark's eyes and spilled out over his cheeks.

A gun? I'd always heard the sounds of gunshots while I was falling asleep at night. Sometimes South Phoenix was a dangerous place, but I'd never seen a gun before that night. Was it real? Was it actually happening? Javi and I had been best friends since the day my family moved into our house, but in all that time, I'd never once seen him naked. When we'd played house sometimes, we'd lain next to each other, cuddling liked we'd seen our parents do, like we were husband and wife. But I'd never had a penis in my mouth before. Okay, so Mr. S had said we were going to play the adult version. I didn't know adults did this. I don't think Javi had ever seen me cry before.

This was a first for both of us. I think.

"Javi! It's your turn. Get on your knees and

suck Mark's penis like a good boy." Mr. S glared at me. "And get those tears out of your eyes," he growled.

Mark's penis began to harden, something he'd never seen or felt before.

I was just six years old, without a single sexual bone in my little body—until that moment was forced upon me.

His body reacted in a manner totally out of the ordinary for him. He started to become aroused, and seeing him in that state sparked something in Javi, and he too experienced arousal.

The sound of a zipper was so loud in Mark's ear. Mr. S grabbed his head. "It's *my* turn to have some fun now." He had both boys on their knees in front of him while he dangled his penis before them, forcing them to take it in turns pleasuring him.

It was a nightmarish circle.

Mark with Mr. S in his mouth while Javi sucked Mark's penis. Javi with his dad's penis in his mouth while Mark sucked off Javi. And so it went on, back and forth for close to an hour. Then Mr. S released his sperm into Mark's mouth, forcing it down his throat. No sooner had he finished than Mark threw up over the floor, tears pouring from him as they never had before. A rush of emotions flooded through him: guilt, shame, embarrassment, fear, hate…

He had no control.

I was forced to shower and wash my face so my tears could no longer be traced on my cheeks. I got home where I was only able to finish half of my dinner, then I went to bed. I cried and shivered through the warm night. My tears could be heard through the walls into my parents' bedroom. My parents came rushing in to see what was wrong. I couldn't tell them the truth. If I did that, I would die. I didn't want to die. So I told them my legs were hurting. My mom explained that I was having growing pains and I would be taller soon. I knew better. My life had just changed irrevocably. No more fun and games. No more imagination and creativity.

Life was real and I had no control over what was to come.

The innocence of two young, fragile bodies was stolen. The world those boys inhabited was no longer the same. Their former world of childhood, innocent games and simple joys was never to exist again.

Day Two - Liver Doctor

"Mr. Land."

"Mr. *Land*."

I opened my eyes slowly to find a man in a white coat standing over my bed. I must have fallen asleep writing after my early morning session of being pricked and poked, and not in the good way.

"Mr. Land, my name is Dr. Rosenswag and I will be your liver specialist for the duration of your treatment. I have some very concerning news about your liver that may be hard to hear."

Hard to hear? That could only mean I was dying, right?

"I have placed you on an emergency liver transplant list and if your enzyme levels get any worse we will be transferring you to another hospital and performing a liver replacement surgery."

I wasn't quite sure what he was saying. My liver was bad?

"You have gone into acute liver failure. You are on the cusp of going into complete failure and if that happens you can die. We are going to do everything in our power to keep that from happening, but you have to understand that if your liver gets worse while in this hospital, we don't have a way to do the transplant. We will have to transfer you to another hospital to make that happen, so we will be keeping

very close eyes on your blood work to make sure you are only moving in the right direction."

I thought I'd been terrified before. How the hell could I be terrified? The morphine was supposed to help me *not* feel, right?

"In order to help your liver heal at a more rapid rate we must keep you on a liquid diet, we will watch your enzymes day by day and begin to add solid foods when we get below the danger zone."

Well, there went my diet.

You'll have to forgive me for going off on a tangent here, but this was *huge*.

Growing up, fitness and health were always a topic of conversation but never a serious one. When the basics of life cost so much, a healthy lifestyle took second place. My family didn't have much money, and most of the time 'going out to eat' meant the drive-through at one of the many local fast-food chains.

I was a competitive athlete in track and field, and I always did what I could to maintain my personal health, in spite of the choices my family was forced to make when it came to feeding everyone. Don't get me wrong—my family had many meals out at nice restaurants, and my mom can cook like no other. Health was just never a real option, or at least that was what we thought.

There are many things that I love, for which I take great responsibility:

Running

Weight Lifting

Dancing

Nutrition

Cooking

Good food cost a great amount of money but my overall health was more important than the price of food. I made a new commitment to my personal health and fitness as soon as I moved out of my parents' house, because *I matter* and I deserve to feel good, look good, and live a long life.

So I made a few decisions.

NO MORE: fast-food, fried food.

A lot LESS: sugar, desserts, dairy products.

And MORE: fruit, veggies, chicken, brown rice, and home cooked meals.

Health and fitness has been proven to have a positive effect on mental and emotional well-being. I always told myself, "Take responsibility for you, take care of you and you will find that your life will get better."

Napoleon Hill (an American author of personal-success literature) came out with a few truths that have come to represent my life:

"Great Reward comes with Great Sacrifice. What are you willing to sacrifice?"

"Great achievement is usually born of great sacrifice, and is never the result of selfishness."

"Strength and growth come only through continuous effort and struggle."

I will succeed. I am determined. I may fall but I

will get up. Life is worth more than the struggles we face. I will overcome, because I am worth it.

I had to remind myself of this, and wonder how I got to this place, because suddenly I was going to be stuck on Jell-O, water and ice cubes until further notice. How the hell did eating Mexican food bring me to *that* point?

In my mind I chanted. *I hereby declare that I will never again eat Mexican food in a place that is not primarily Mexican, nor will I eat Mexican food from a restaurant that does not have Mexican cooks, nor will I eat Mexican food in a state that does not border Mexico.*

I was covering all bases.

I reached for my phone to call my mother to give her the news and of course, I couldn't resist taking a selfie in my *beautiful* hospital gown. Yeah, cue eye-roll.

But I stopped when I noticed my veins popping out of my arm, like my skin was tighter than a woman who had had Botox consistently for 10 years. I had never seen so many veins in one place. I stared at my arm for what felt like an hour, just thinking about rivers and birds and life, and how my very existence depended on the blood running through my veins. My thoughts veered from peace and the earth, to how I wanted to be buried if I did end up dying there in the hospital.

My head began to feel heavy and I rolled over to watch the nurse push another vial of morphine into

my veins. My mind stayed on these life thoughts even while my eyes closed, and I gripped the edge of the bed as my body began to warm from the morphine.

I was high again. I felt like I was flying next to the birds, gazing down at the treetops and feeling the wind beneath me. I felt so peaceful, like I was floating, yet I was still terrified. I lay there in my bed, tears rolling down my cheeks and I had no clue why.

Was I afraid of dying?

How could I be afraid of dying when I'd prayed over and over for God to take my life so I wouldn't have to deal with all of this pain? I thought I was at peace, that I'd come to terms with the idea of death. Was this the morphine again?

Then I realized why I was crying.

I was mourning the loss of something precious. My tears were for the little boy who was robbed so cruelly of something that should have been his to give.

Only it wasn't given. It was taken, in pain and tears and blood.

~ 0 ~

December 1995

That was a night Mark would never forget. There he and Javi were, back in the 'dungeon'—the torture chamber of Mr. S's home. They walked into the room and it was set up the same way it had always been, even down to the milk and cookies on the table next to the bed.

Mr. S walked into the room. "Okay, you two,

That the vile act was repeated over and over throughout the following two and a half years was nothing short of monstrous.

It was then that Mark's life began to follow a pattern.

~ 0 ~

I closed my notepad and put down my pen, I needed a second to reflect on myself. It was difficult to write, and even more difficult to write about oneself. Yes, I used a name that was not completely mine but the story I was telling was the life I lived.

I smiled every day and put on this happy face. How can I explain? It's as if every day of my life I went out in drag but with no wig, no makeup, no dresses and no heels. My drag was to hide my true self, my emotions, and my inability to forget.

I lay there in that hospital bed, tears rolling down my face. The morphine had allowed my emotions to run rampant and I had no control over them. My body felt warm, the morphine flowing through me as I sank into the pillows. I felt safe. My eyelids were heavy and...

I knew no more.

Day Two - Morphine & Shadows

A diet consisting solely of liquids and Jell-O didn't keep my hunger at bay; the growls would wake me up, they were so loud.

There were other things that woke me up, too.

The morphine was really messing me up. My eyelids felt so heavy as I tried to open my eyes, but once they were open, everything was just that little bit… strange. First, there was the smoke coming from smoke stacks in town, but in *my* reality/state of mind, I saw flying railway trains.

My eyesight grew filmy, like I was seeing through gauze, as my body tried to shut down and let me sleep. The construction on the hospital wing taking place outside my window *really* wasn't helping. The construction workers worked right outside my window; if the blinds were open we could stare at each other. Yeah, it was kind of creepy. What was even *creepier*? It took me a while to realize the construction workers were human, because for a while there, I thought I was watching TV, with Bob the Builder and his crew of talking tools….

Yeah, so I wasn't *that* far off.

The way the morphine was playing tricks with my eyes reminded me of the shadows that my sisters used to complain about. The shadows that crept like ghosts through their windows, dark figures who stood

outside at night, stiff as a board, unflinching even when the girls screamed and whimpered.

If they only knew.

Those were not shadows or ghosts. They were Javi's siblings.

~ 0 ~

Mr. S sent his other children out of the house at night, telling them to sit in Mark's yard so that they could not witness the screams and tears of the boys who were being abused and dominated in the back room. The children stood with looks of horror on their faces, as if they had experienced the very thing that was happening that moment in their home next door.

A knock on the window of Mark's bedroom would send his heart into overdrive. There was the man, the shadow of the devil himself, standing in silence, waiting without patience. The gun in his hand was always visible so that there would be no question of games. Mark knew that he had to do as he was told.

Mark crawled out of his window and followed Mr. S to their home next door. As the walk of torture took place, the shadows of children filled the back yard and stared into the Landry home as if they were the home security system.

Mark knew what was about to happen. His young fragile body would be taken again and he had no other options, no control over the outcome. The choice was simple; live and feel the pain, or die and never feel anything again.

It was better for me to suffer the pain than anyone else in my family. I would not be able to survive knowing that one of my sisters or brothers suffered the same torment that I did. I often wondered if Javi and I were the only ones Mr. S abused, molested, raped, and tortured.

The shadows that reflected into the girls' window were dark shadows of fear, danger and warning, yet they could not heed their calling; their lives were also on the line.

In church Mark heard ministers preaching about losing your virginity and having sex before marriage, and how sinful it was.

I prayed harder every day for God to fix me and to end this abuse. I hated this man for taking my virginity and for paving my one-way ticket to hell. I was young and didn't know any better, but I was not going to let this man ruin my life.

Mark was always taught from the good old Gospel of the King James Bible, the Bible that states a man who rapes should marry his victim.

And what if the victim was a child? What then?

It was then that the flashbacks began: the same shadows that fell each night crept into Mark's mind.

Smells, certain sensations of emptiness, colors, sounds and the voices of men—all of them sent a live

feed of video footage through Mark's mind. He could hear the screams of his own voice as if he was still in that vile room. He could hear the moans of Mr. S as his pleasures were fulfilled.

Random tears fell in random places, with no way to explain why to those who questioned them.

Mark was terrified of men. He became attached to his mother, never leaving her side. Mrs. Landry would go to the nail salon and Mark was there by her side. A trip to the grocery store and he was there too. He sat practically in her lap at church. His body became overwhelmed with fear and self-hatred.

Imagine being six years old and having a grown man tearing into your body with his manhood.

I prayed that God would take me far, far away, anywhere *but that place of pain. I knew God wouldn't give me more than I can handle but I didn't feel strong enough for this.*

Mark had no one to talk to. He couldn't talk to Javi because it reminded him of reality. He couldn't talk to his family because if he did so, they would all die. So Mark talked to God.

It didn't matter if God was listening or not. At least he was someone to talk to.

~ 0 ~

David was finally off work and back at the hospital. He could tell I'd been writing; my emotions could be read all over my face and God knew, I'd

gone through most of them that day.

I made room on the bed for him so he could hold me and we could talk about our day. First of all, I had to tell him about the liver specialist and the news I'd received.

When it came time to tell him the flashbacks, it was easier to let him read than to relive it all over again. His face tightened, but he held my hand as he turned the pages.

We sat and watched HGTV. Not only was it my favorite channel, it was the only good channel that had reception in the hospital. We enjoyed the time together, sitting quietly. I felt safe, I felt loved and I fell fast asleep in his arms.

This was my first overnight stay in a hospital. By night two it was starting to get to me. I woke up and David was gone. The pain was finally dissipating and I was starting to feel better. I just wanted to be in my own bed.

I called for the nurse to ask for water, and asked how much longer she thought I'd have to stay there. Her reply made my heart sink.

"You'll be here a few more days yet."

A few more days. *A few more days*. UGH.

I'd known, of course. There was no way, after hearing the liver doctor, that I was going to get out any sooner than that, but somehow hearing it out loud was worse. Why did I even ask?

"God, what is happening to me? I'm always in good health. I take care of my body as much as

possible. I go to the gym, I eat healthily. What am I doing wrong?"

Wait…

I was talking to God again.

I remember the last time I talked to God, the last thing I ever prayed.

I remembered it like it was yesterday.

My last prayer rang through my head, and I began falling, falling, faster and faster, until I found myself standing in the room, back in November of 2011, watching myself attempt suicide—and fail.

"God, thank you for not taking my life, but why would you save me when everyone around me says you don't love me because I am gay? Why would you save my life when I am an abomination in your eyes? God, please, tell me what I am supposed to do. The life I have lived during my existence on this earth only contradicts everything I have been taught. I know you made me who I am, you made me the man I am, but if you made me this way, then why do you hate me? I just tried to take my own life. How come no one saw this coming? How come *no one* has seen how much pain I'm in? I have never been at peace my entire life. I'm not even sure what it means to be at peace. God, please—help me."

I saw myself climbing off the table, removing the rope from around my neck and kneeling next to my bed, holding my dog Layla and praying my last prayer.

Layla was so much more than just a dog.

Layla saved my life.

She wasn't even allowed in my little studio apartment, but she was quiet and didn't make much noise. She held down the fort and was so peaceful. But that night? She barked as I'd never heard her before, loudly and continuously. I could have been kicked out if the landlord had heard her. She was relentless, jumping up to the table, a thing she had also never done before.

Layla was my angel. Like I said, she saved my life. But I was still in pain. Still trying to find my way out of that pain.

I did the only thing I could think of. I made a video.

I lay there in that hospital bed, like I was there back in 2011 watching myself open my laptop and turn on my webcam.

I watched myself cry, my grief overwhelming. I spilled out my heartache and pain, the camera recording it all while I talked without any care of who would see the video or how people would react to it.

I was coming out. I was talking about my experiences with sexual abuse, *finally* saying out loud all of the things I'd kept within my heart for thirteen long years. I was finally saying it all out loud, releasing all of the pain I'd held inside my whole life.

I watched myself from my hospital bed as I sat there at the dining table in Oregon and talked, nothing held back, nothing left untold. My story was released for the first time. I didn't have to carry it alone

anymore.

I sat there for an hour and recorded myself pouring my heart onto the world wide web, hoping that someone would care enough eventually to watch it and help me carry those burdens.

When the hour long video was complete, recorded, saved and burned to a disk, I shut my laptop and fell asleep holding Layla. She was all I had.

Day Three - Fighting Back

1997

The bell rang. Time for class, so Mark ran as fast as he could to make it on time.

There were three bells. There was the first one that signaled the start of the stampede as children rushed to their assigned rooms, another to warn that time was running out and the last to announce that *hey, if you're not inside by now? You're late.*

During morning recess Mark always played with his friends in the field furthest away from their classroom, yet they would always make it back just in the nick of time.

That particular day Mark was filled with a sense of bravery. He wasn't alone—Javi felt it too, almost as though a sudden burst of testosterone flooded their bodies, making them feel like the sons of superman. They talked big and walked around the school like they owned the place, although both of them were unsure as to the source of this newfound confidence.

When it was time for lunch, they talked, and both were in agreement—they were done being tortured and abused. Their confidence was increasing in leaps and bounds, so much so that they came up with a plan.

They were going to fight back.

They talked it over until it was once again time

for class. After school was over, they went their separate ways to prepare for the night of their lives.

As planned, Javi went into the room while Mr. S was out of the house, to hide knives between the mattresses.

They had it all planned. They were going to kill Mr. S.

When Mark got to the house that night, he and Javi went back to the room and sat there, waiting for Mr. S to arrive. Mark's heart was pounding, his throat dry as a bone and his hands trembling. Javi was clearly in a similar state. Mark kept up the silent prayer in his head.

"God, please, let us be able to pull this off."

Mr. S walked into the room. "Take off your clothes."

Mark tried to keep his voice even. "No, we have something else planned."

Mr. S appeared a little confused, unsurprisingly. "What exactly do you two have planned?"

Javi looked to Mark, who took a deep breath. "You… you need to get naked and lie on the bed. We're going to do a magic trick."

To their relief he agreed to participate.

They tied both his arms to the side posts on the bed, but when they went to tie his feet, they went between the mattresses to grab the knives.

They weren't there.

Mark and Javi looked up and there he stood with the ropes in one hand and the knives in the other.

Mark had no clue how he got the knives, but Mr. S
was pissed and suddenly they were scared more than
ever.

Everything he had put them through up until
that point seemed like a bad dream, compared to what
followed.

As far as Mark was concerned, *that* was a
nightmare.

He grabbed Mark, tearing the clothes from his
body, and proceeded to rape him.

Mark had never been in such pain. Pinning him
to the bed, Mr. S tied up Javi and made Mark suck his
penis, not once letting go of them. Mark tried fighting
him off, yelling as loudly as he could.

"Please stop!"

"Please!"

Tears fell down his face, and it seemed like the
life was being sucked out of him, his body
weakening, and there was nothing he could do about
it.

Then Mr. S hit Mark in his stomach. After that
Mark felt nothing as he began lose consciousness,
Javi's screams echoing inside his head.

He would never forget those screams as long as
he lived.

There was to be no reprieve. When Mark came
to, the night of torture continued. With hindsight,
Mark doubted it lasted longer than usual, but in his
mind it felt like it went on forever.

The next morning his mom came to Mark's

room to wake the kids up for school.

Mark kept complaining that his stomach hurt. He ached to tell her the truth but couldn't. There was no way he'd risk the lives of everyone he loved. Instead, he told her he thought he had diarrhea, and she made him stay home from school that day.

The previous night was a blur. He didn't remember how he'd gotten home. He didn't remember how Javi had ended up, and he certainly didn't remember how that horrific night had ended. All he knew was that he was in a lot of pain, his stomach was beginning to bruise and there was no way he was letting anyone see that.

Mark became very sneaky when it came to changing for bed. From that point on he would never let anyone see him with his shirt off. He became very insecure and protective of himself.

In the summer, he swam with his shirt on. He made sure the door was locked and secure when using the restroom or shower. In the winter when they used the hot tub, he made sure his shirt stayed on then, too. After school sometimes they played baseball, football, or basketball, and it was usually shirts versus skins. Mark made sure that any team he played on, kept their shirts on.

It had been the first time—and sometimes it felt like the last time—that Mark had truly tried to fight. But that night knocked the confidence right out of him, and it was something he never saw again.

In a way I still have to fight back. I'm fighting every day. I'm continuously fighting myself—my mind and my emotions. Maybe one day I'll be able to fight for every person who has had their voice silenced by abuse.

Sometimes I get a knot or cramps in my stomach, and the pain will remind me of the day I tried to fight for myself. Those small, painful gestures make me feel weak and sometimes make me feel less of a man.

It's a funny thing. Even eighteen years later, I can't seem hide from the torture of my past.

~ 0 ~

The painful sigh was jerked out of me. *Ugh.*

I felt something clamp down on my finger and my eyes jolted open. The tightening around my chest eased when I realized it was just the nurse waking me yet again. Time to weigh me and take more blood.

My heartbeat was still racing, however, when I asked her, "Is it four a.m. already?"

She grasped my hand gently. "Yes, dear. Just relax. We didn't mean to startle you."

One change though: I was able to stand on my own while they took my weight. I weighed fourteen pounds less than the day I arrived in the hospital.

God, that was only three days ago.

I still felt weak but there was less pain. The nurse informed me that I was no longer allowed to have the morphine, and that I was being switched over to naproxen for the pain.

Great. No more high. No more seeing a distorted reality. It was back to the boring old blank walls of the hospital and HGTV.

I think I preferred the distorted reality. Because in the real world, I had a roommate.

A roommate who was currently shouting at the top of his lungs. "Nurse! Nurse! Nurse, damn it!"

The nurse came running in. "Mr. Sanders, what's wrong?"

"I shit myself and I think I wet the bed."

My roommate was an older gentleman, probably in his mid to late seventies. He had no visitors and spoke loudly. Having said that, I can't recall the times he tried to have a conversation with me; I was either half asleep or the morphine kept me focused on... other things.

It was about six a.m. and a team of nurses came in to change out Mr. Sanders's sheets and bed. All I could hear was Mr. Sanders talking to himself from behind the curtain that separated us.

'How does a man at my age lose control of his bowels?'

'I haven't shit myself since I was four years old. And I haven't pissed myself since I was seven.'

'I can't even imagine living like this. Hell, I can't even look at myself in the mirror after that.'

I sat in my bed, my eyes full with tears.

It's not easy to admit that I've spent most of my life wetting the bed. Yes, I was 'potty trained', but that wasn't the issue. I was just terrified to get up and

go.

Fifteen years old. That is how old I was before I stopped consistently peeing the bed. Between the ages of fifteen and twenty-five I have on rare occasions peed the bed when I was triggered into flashbacks or blackouts.

It was horrible. Imagine having a sleep-over with friends, either at their houses or at home, and not being able to sleep because you are terrified you're going to wake up in a puddle and everyone at school or at church would soon find out that you're a 'bed wetter'. Imagine being on camping trips in the middle of the forest, and having to go out of your tent all by yourself into pitch black darkness to pee three or four times a night. And desperately trying not to wake up everyone else because you are afraid you're going to pee and get everyone wet.

It was so embarrassing. Once the sun was up I would try to get out of bed before everyone else, throw my sheets in the washing machine and flip my mattress so that no one would notice, but of course there was the smell that filled the room. That could never be hidden. I would go to the bathroom to shower and clean off, and I would look at myself in the mirror and cry. My mind would berate me, calling me every negative thing it could. That way, when my family did it, there was less hurt because I'd said it first.

There are only so many times you can flip a mattress before the stains become very obvious.

Sometimes I'd pee while fast asleep, at other times I would be wide awake but just too afraid to get up. I'd hold it in until it hurt and I had no choice but to let it out.

People used to call me pee body and bed wetter. I'd find a closet to hide in and cry, or I'd lock myself in my room or climb a tree, just to get away from everyone. I was afraid. NOT lazy—there is a huge difference between the two. People assumed I peed the bed because I was too lazy to get up and go to the bathroom, or because I was dreaming I was in the bathroom and it just… happened. That was not the case.

Take a look at the statistics; peeing the bed as a young adult can be a symptom of PTSD.

Instead of reaching out to help, people made fun of me, which only made things worse. How could I begin to talk about *anything*, share what was really going on, when before I could say anything, people made *fun* of me?

I understood what Mr. Sanders was going through. I knew what he was feeling only too well.

He walked over and peeked around the curtain that divided the room, his cheeks pink. "Did you hear any of what I said? Did you smell anything?"

I kept my voice soft. "Mr. Sanders, there's no shame in what happened, trust me. Life takes us on journeys and challenges us, but it's not the battle that shapes us, it's how we react to it. Don't let this bring you down. I'm certainly not going to judge you."

Then I grinned. "If anything, you're lucky. *I* haven't been able to poop for two days."

We sat there and laughed while the nurses finished up the cleaning process. Inwardly I rejoiced that I'd put a smile on his face.

I was sinking back into a light sleep just as David walked into the room. I tried to keep my eyes open to see him but the morning had taken all my energy. When I awoke, a wonderful aroma tickled my nostrils, and I knew instantly what it was. My first real breakfast since I'd been admitted. But when I saw it, I couldn't believe my eyes.

Eggs, sausage, and a pancake. *Sausage.* My mouth drooled at the thought of eating meat again.

Yeah, okay, so obviously I'm no vegan.

Unfortunately it was not meant to be. Someone had made a mistake, and I'd been brought the wrong food. I watched in dismay as it was taken away, to be replaced with Jell-O, and ginger ale.

At least they gave me *two* cups of Jell-O that time. Whoop-de-doo.

But the smell of that sausage made me remember the time we'd spent spring break in Texas, barbequing with the family and just having the time of our lives.

Day Three – Memories

It was a month before Mark turned seven. Mark's family celebrated his birthday early during spring break by taking the family to Texas to visit Mr. Landry's side of the family. This trip was unforgettable because Mark met a lot of family members that he had never met before, and he learned how to shoot a gun.

That was fun. The men of the family went out and shot at these flying disks made of clay, not to mention soda cans. The whole time Mark had that gun in his hands, all he could think of was how great it would be to shoot Mr. S. Except, of course, Mark didn't have a gun back home. Going out shooting was so great because Mark had a day of bonding with his brother, his cousins, and his dad and his brothers. They stayed out for about six hours shooting, and every hour they were out Mark got better and better with his aim. Mark's uncle was so impressed; he went to the car and pulled out a bow and arrow to see what the kids could do with that.

Oh, was Mark excited!

He took that bow and arrow and hit everything he aimed at. Well, maybe not *everything*. The thoughts of killing Mr. S just kept ringing in Mark's head. He kept thinking how easy it would be to make one of the bows and then as an arrow he could use

knifes or something. The thoughts just repeated over and over in his head.

Looking back, it makes me sad. There I was, having a great time with my family, and that bastard was still there, like a cancer in my mind.

Later that week Mark's family went to their first theme park, Six Flags. It was *amazing*. The park was huge and it was so full of fun, life and happy people. All they had in Arizona was this small, ancient theme park with small, uninspiring roller coasters, and after an hour you were done with everything and ready to go home. Mark could have spent a *week* in Six Flags and not have seen everything, he was in love!

For the birthday party the whole family showed up, which was saying something, because the Landry family was very large. Well, they do say everything is bigger in Texas and the size of this family proved that to be true. Everyone brought food to share, but best of all they brought gifts. The food was amazing; there were so many things Mark had never eaten before. Mrs. Landry made her all-time famous chili dip, and grandma made the most amazing home-made biscuits and elk sausage. Mark's aunts and uncles all brought their family dishes, like wild boar, elk, and deer. Everything was cooked to perfection and no one could have asked for better food. Mark was finally able to taste dishes from his 'southern roots' and was

put in a food coma (that feeling you get when you eat too much and just want to sleep) the entire week.

Of course, all good things must come to an end eventually.

Spring break was over, the Landry family went back home and got ready to go back to school. Mark was so excited to go home because he got to see his friends.

Mark's family arrived home on Friday, and that night Tony and Mark spent the night at Geo's house just so they could all hang out and catch up before school started again. They watched three movies, ate a ton of food and told each other stories about spring break. Geo told all about how he'd gotten to see his grandma, and had gone fishing and camping with his dad and his cousins. Tony told all about how his dad was getting a pool built into his back yard; Geo and Mark were so excited because they never had anywhere to swim before that point. When it was Mark's turn, he shared it all; the guns, the bow & arrows, the food and especially Six Flags.

It had been the first week since Marks was six years old that he hadn't been abused once. At the time, it felt like the best week of his life.

Texas. Who would have thought it could be a place of escape? Even if it had only been for a week, escape was truly what it was.

~ 0 ~

I had been getting texts from my former roomies, checking up on me, and of course I told

them to come see me. We had plans for them to join me for lunch, to see for themselves what these chefs called *food* in that place.

It was finally time for lunch and my diet was still restricted, so I ate Jell-O and a popsicle and drank ginger ale, tortured by the heavenly aroma of Donald and Brad's lunch. Donald's chicken fingers smelt *amazing* and Brad's cheese burger made my stomach *beg* for something savory.

Those boys were two of the best roommates I could have ever asked for. They were there for me like family and it was so damn good to see their faces. The few hours we shared in that hospital room, just talking and catching up, made me feel so much better, especially after the morning I'd had.

See, I met those boys through a gig we were all working. We almost ended up hooking up...

Well, Donald and I did, a little, but the connection we had was special and we hit it off like sisters. We'd maintained that relationship and nothing else really transpired besides the amazing friendship that resulted.

Donald and Brad lived in North Carolina when we first met and had been talking about moving to NYC. I happened to have been evicted from my apartment, thanks to my roommate not paying the rent for six months, so I was couch surfing.

The timing was just perfect and we became roommates. I could probably write a book about the things we did, and if the walls could talk we could

write a series. It was possibly the best time of my life.

When it came time for them to leave the hospital, I reminded them of how much I appreciated them, how much I loved them for everything they did for me.

After the boys had left I turned the T.V. back on, and there was a commercial about a talent agency looking for new young talent.

I started to laugh.

When I was eight years old, I called a talent agency from a commercial just like this one and I made myself an appointment for an audition. After I hung up the phone, I ran to my mom.

"Mom, what are headshots?"

She peered at me, clearly puzzled. "Why do you ask?"

"Because I need some to take with me to my audition," I explained.

"Audition? What audition?" Her face was a picture of confusion.

I was bursting with pride. "I made an appointment with a talent agency because I want to be a movie star one day."

She must have thought I was crazy, but she encouraged me and agreed to take me to the appointment.

When we arrived, we were greeted like we were royalty, handed a bottle of water and escorted to sit down with one of the agents.

When the first question was about finances, my

heart sank and I knew it wasn't going to happen. They wanted $800 per class for acting and singing classes.

I had thought this was an audition where I could showcase my skills, and be taken in and given work. I was eight years old. I had no idea how difficult it really was.

My dreams of being a movie star were taken away because we were poor. Unsurprisingly, I gave up on acting.

Acting. Movie star…

Just like that, I was back in the dungeon.

Remember those boxes I talked about, that sat in the closet with "MEDIA" written on the side?

Well, that day the boxes were empty.

The equipment they'd contained was already set up.

Day Three - Movie Stars

Summer, 1997

It was 11:15p.m. and there he was, Mr. S, standing at Mark's window.

Mark went over and opened it. "You need to leave right now or I will scream as loud as I can," he whispered. Mark's brothers remained asleep in their beds.

Why me? There were four of them in the room at the time, but Mr. S always only wanted Mark. He pulled out his gun, and of course Mark climbed out of the window and followed him to his house.

As they walked into the room, it was obvious something was different. The bed was in the same place, the nightstand too. The windows were still shut, the dark curtains covering the boards on the windows to keep the room from looking like the prison it was. The media box that had once sat in the closet was opened and empty. The room was brightly lit like a movie set; lights and a video camera aimed at the bed.

Javi was already on the bed, tied up.

Mr. S untied Javi and demanded that they get naked. Before they'd finished, the camera began to roll, with Mr. S yelling out commands.

"Kiss! … With tongue ... That's perfect."

"Now off with the clothes … Take his shirt

off… Now keep kissing … Now his shoes… More kissing … Pants off … More kissing… "

Mark's tears began to fall. Almost three years of this, three years of pain, fear, and hate, and suddenly their torturer was capturing it all on camera so he could pleasure himself to it when they were gone. Foreboding filled him.

'We're going to die today.' The words played over and over in his head. He couldn't hear, couldn't think and his vision began to blur as his body started going into shock.

Mr. S yelled and yanked him back into harsh reality. "Get it together, you're not done here." He began firing off more instructions that blurred into one another. "Okay, more kissing … take off his underwear … more kissing …. Hold each other's faces … run your hands over each other's bodies… Kiss and get each other hard … perfect, keep that up for a bit. Mark, now you suck Javi… "

Mark's body began to jerk and tense up, about to cum.

Mr. S yelled, "Not yet!" A second later he was majorly pissed.

Mark ejaculated for the very first time but Mr. S wasn't ready for it. Mark had ruined the film. Mr. S grabbed the camera and threw it across the room, then grabbed Mark and pushed him over the bed, instructing Javi to penetrate him.

Something of his father's mood had apparently rubbed off on Javi, only he seemed to be taking out

Just before the start of the new school year, Mark's family received notice that the landlord's daughter was getting married and the house would be given to her as a wedding gift. The Landry family was forced to pack up and move, and just like that, the abuse was over.

The family was forced to live with friends and family members until Mark's dad was able to save enough to get them into a home again. This also meant the kids would be forced out of school until they had a more permanent place to lay their heads.

A few months into the house search, Mark's parents found a beautiful three-level home and they moved all of their belongings into the garage. They were all prepared for the move, until the day before when they were told that his parents' credit was too bad to buy the house. And so the search continued.

Late into winter, the Landry family finally found a house in northwest Phoenix, a complete turn-around compared to the little pink house where they'd lived before. This house was two stories high, with four bedrooms and three bathrooms, so much bigger than any previous home, and it was all theirs. The Landry family qualified to buy the house through the Hud program (A government based program for low income families that resells houses after they had been foreclosed or abandoned). They moved in three weeks after the bad news on the last house.

A week after being in the new house, all the kids started a new school and made new friends.

Mark was starting the fourth grade, and his teachers loved him and helped him fit right in. He started running track and field, and he was good, so fast that no one could beat him. He ran every day, even during recess. He found that running helped keep all his problems out of his mind, allowing him to relax and do something he found fun at the same time.

Moving into the new house felt like a good start to a new life. Mark thought he could finally sleep, knowing he was safe and couldn't be hurt by Mr. S any longer. But the night of making the movie haunted him every day. It was *proof*—unless of course, it was miraculously damaged when Mr. S threw the camera across the room—but it was still proof that everything had really happened. Mr. S still had it. The bastard was probably masturbating to it every night since he didn't have Mark there in person any more. Mark wondered if he made more movies with his son and other kids, or if he was satisfied with just Mark's friend. Every night Mark prayed for Javi, hoping that his battle had ended and that he'd been able to survive this nightmare.

To Mr. S they were movie stars. To Mark and Javi, they were tortured. Everyone else only saw happy, loving children.

Why didn't anyone see it?

How in the hell could such obvious things be missed?

~ 0 ~

Knock Knock

The nurses walked in, carrying three vases filled with the most beautiful flowers, a teddy bear and countless balloons. They were gifts from friends who were out of state, unable to visit but wishing to send their love.

I was truly feeling the love.

My life is full of amazing people, always has been. I believe that because of the things I've endured, I naturally attach myself to people who are happy, loving, and caring. I tend to push away those who are the opposite, with ease. I've gone through enough hate and torture. Why would I surround myself with people who will just keep me in that place of torment?

Maybe I should back up and tell you a little bit about myself besides what you already know with all of the abuse.

I was born in Phoenix, Arizona, and raised in a very conservative Christian home. I went to church four or more times a week. I sang as a praise and worship leader. I taught Children's Church, and as a young adult I taught in the youth ministries. I was the lead singer of the youth band. I even released my own Christian album.

I went to two different elementary schools, and in high school I was super involved in everything; track and field Captain: Student Government: Spanish club: photo club: national honor society: Christian club on campus: Fellowship of Christian Athletes: the list went on. I was recognized with honors for being a

student athlete and graduated top of my class. I received scholarships from multiple universities and went to two of them.

I was in a fraternity, sat on boards and committees. I was student body president. I even traveled to conferences where I would lobby members of congress to pass bills.

I helped write legislation that was presented to the floor of the House and Senate.

Do you understand what I'm trying to say here?

On the outside I was the perfect child, the perfect adolescent; I looked the part, acted the part, and my achievements only went to prove it.

But if you peeled away all of those layers that I'd used to hide my true self, to mask the pain and fear that had its grasp on me, you would have found someone completely different.

Yes, of course I love politics, I love singing, I love being in leadership positions but that confident, happy, proud young man was weak, due to no fault of his own.

I dropped out of college after coming out and failing to commit suicide. Life takes a toll on you when you hold onto things. But at the same time, things happen for a reason and timing may not always seem perfect, but it is.

I suffered sexual abuse under one man for three years. I became very good at hiding things, hiding my emotions and creating a façade. I was so good at it that for three years no one, not *one person*, could tell

that I was being raped and threatened, that I was being used as a sex object for a man who got pleasure out of little boys.

How the fuck does that happen?

How does *no one* see the pain?

It only goes to show how blind our world truly is to sexual abuse and the way it affects our children.

Because there *were* times when I exhibited physical signs of abuse, but they went unnoticed. I can almost guess what was said;

He's just a boy. He probably got it playing at school.

He's just a boy. He probably got into a fight.

He probably scraped his knee.

He probably landed on it wrong.

I don't hate my friends and family for not noticing. In fact, I've forgiven them. Little did they know this was just three years of my war, just one battle out of many.

~ 0 ~

During this battle, from the spring of 1995 through to the fall of 1997, Mark and Javi were molested, raped and abused by Mr. S.

It was like clockwork. They would walk into the back room and he would remind them of their death wish if they happened to decide to tell anyone. Then they would get to work.

The memories repeat over and over in my head without warning, no sense of timeline, no care of

*where I am or what I am doing. They just appear
scattered, random, yet vivid.*

*I can remember as if it were yesterday. The
room was dark and cold, filled with emptiness. The
bed sat perfectly centered on the back wall with a
night stand on each side. The dim lamp only lit the
room bright enough for you to see your hands in front
of you. The closet had no doors just boxes sealed on
floor. A black fabric covered the windows to keep the
sun from revealing the secrets of the room.*

Most days the process was the same. The boys
would help each other remove their clothes and
provide each other with service until Mr. S was ready
to be serviced. Slowly, as time went on, they tried
more daring things.

Some days Javi and Mark would mess around
without the interruption of Mr. S. Some days Mr. S
would make one of the boys sit and watch him get
serviced by the other.

Mr. S saw this as entertainment. He would
occasionally put out popcorn and cookies so the boy
who was watching could eat while he watched the
show. *Dinner and a movie.*

The gun was always present to remind the boys
that if they ever told anyone, he would kill them.

The most difficult part of this whole situation
was that as the boys got older, things got easier. The
abuse became routine. It became *normal*. That didn't

mean they liked it. They still cried. They still hated being forced onto each other, but the actions were so normalized to them.

I prayed everyday
"God, KILL this man so that I can live a normal childhood."
"God, ease the pain so I don't have to feel it anymore."
"God, take me away so that I don't have to live in fear."
"God, don't make me gay because I don't want to lose my family."
"God, kill me, please. I can't take the pain anymore."

Javi and Mark lived a life that no child should ever have to live. These boys were abused for three years, unable to trust anyone enough to tell them because their fear was greater than trust. The hope was always there; maybe *someone* would notice so the boys wouldn't have to say anything.

No one saw past my tears.
No one heard my prayers.
No one heard my cries at night and no one saw the scars I was hiding.
I was afraid of dying so I couldn't tell anyone.

This was war.

Not the kind of war you read about in history class, not the kind of war that had an end or strategic planning. This war was one that would haunt and torment Javi and Mark for the rest of their lives.

Mark was forced to go to church at least four days a week, where he would pray and beg God to intervene. Mark turned to music and began to sing, hoping that someone would hear the pain in his heart through his voice. Tears would fall down his face as he sang on the platform in front of the hundred or so people that were in the congregation.

"Amazing grace, how sweet the sound that saved a wretch like me."

"God has smiled on me, I want the world to know that God has smiled on me."

"I'm on the battlefield for my Lord, I promised him I would serve him till I die."

Mark's battlefield was the streets where he grew up, the church he attended, the friends and family he thought he could lean on and trust. His battlefield consisted of holding onto pain and fear, with no possibility of victory in battle.

This one battle started a war in Mark's heart, a questioning of everything and everyone.

How could he live? How could he survive? That he did was a miracle in itself.

The sad part?

Mr. S was not the only one. Not by a long shot.

~ 0 ~

It was time for dinner. David was sitting at my bedside, just watching me write and think.

I wonder what he thought I was writing, based on my facial expressions.

David had gotten himself lasagna from the hospital cafeteria and I was prepared for yet another meal made of gelatin.

When my doctor walked in with the lady who served the food, I sat up.

"You are getting normal food today, but please, eat slowly. Take your time and don't eat too much of the meat."

I was so happy I could cry. I got a turkey burger, French fries and ginger ale.

Then it hit me: this meant my enzyme levels were out of the danger zone. Joy overwhelmed me and tears fell down my cheeks.

For the first time ever, David cried in front of me, clearly experiencing the same happiness I felt.

We ate, but I was only able to finish half the meal before I was full. It took me about an hour to eat half, though a few of the bites made me nauseous and I had to take it easy.

Finally it was time for David to go and time for me to fall asleep. The food had put me into the happiest food-coma ever.

Day Four – Family Matters

It was 3:30 a.m. and I was awake: I think my body was becoming accustomed to the 4.00 a.m. procedures. I dimmed my light and looked around for my phone so I could play a game of solitaire before the nurses came in. I usually made sure to do the daily challenge every single day, but I had missed a few of them, being sick and all.

When I turned over, I noticed that the bed next to me was empty. The curtain was drawn back, the bathroom door was open but Mr. Sanders was not in the room.

When the nurses came in at four o'clock, I questioned them as to his whereabouts.

"Mr. Sanders was transferred into his own private room because he has become contagious. We are going to be taking an extra vial of blood today to make sure you did not get what he has."

Great. Now the thoughts were rolling around inside my head. *What if I got it and I get worse and they keep me longer?* A sanitation team came in and scrubbed his side of the room. Then they wiped down everything in the whole room, had me shower while they changed the bedding on my bed, and mopped the floors.

Whatever Mr. Sanders had must have been pretty bad for them to bring in a full sanitation team. I

was too scared to ask, fearing I wouldn't like the answer—not that they would have told me anyway.

About twenty minutes after the cleaning was complete, my new roommate, Mr. Frankford, appeared. He was also an older man, maybe a little older than Mr. Sanders. He didn't look so well. There were hoses and wires attached to him everywhere. He also has no control over his bowels.

Mr. Sanders had had no visitors. Kelsie, Mr. Frankford's granddaughter, stayed with him the entire time. He didn't always remember who she was, but somehow she figured out that he could remember whenever she sang to him. Her voice was incredible.

I did not mind the serenading in the slightest.

It must have seemed pretty strange to an onlooker. They would be in mid conversation and he would ask her who she is. She would start singing and within a minute he knew exactly where they were in their conversation. The mind is an amazing thing.

She should have been his doctor.

The way Kelsie cared for Mr. Frankford made me miss my family.

My family is and has always been super close. We are very affectionate and loving, something that I missed.

Yes, David and I were affectionate, but it was different.

I grew up in a family where if there was a family in need, you helped them in any way you could. If that was with a hug or a smile, great. If it

was with groceries, fine. I was taught to serve and love people.

~ 0 ~

Mark's dad was a minister, and part of his ministry was keeping kids off the streets. Kids would come through their house who had been abandoned by their families, or whose families couldn't take care of them anymore. Sometimes they were drug addicts, needing a way out. These kids would stay with the family, and they would feed them, clothe them and keep them off the streets.

Mark and his brother and sisters called them their 'adopted siblings.'

They lived with Mark's family periodically, some for weeks at a time, and others for months or years. They became a part of the family who worked together to help them kick their addictions, which ranged from sex to drugs to alcohol. Nevertheless, Mark called them family.

Ray Ray was one such 'sibling' and he would always stick in Mark's mind, for all the wrong reasons.

Ray Ray was a well-known drug addict and dealer in Phoenix. He was in and out of addiction facilities, their home, and constantly getting in trouble with the law. He lived with Mark's family as a favor to the pastor of the church they attended because he was the pastor's nephew. But he was bad news. He would come and go out of the house as he pleased, reeking of marijuana, and you could tell he'd just had

a fix of *something*. His drug tests would show he had been addicted to meth, cocaine, ecstasy and many other things. Mark could remember his dad, weak and barely able to move because he had been sick, yet finding enough energy in his body to tackle Ray Ray to the ground after he came home once with drugs in his pockets and smelling of the streets. Ray Ray was secretly sneaking around with one of Mark's sisters, and had convinced her that he was the man of her dreams. He almost ruined her life.

Ray Ray wasn't just bad news for Mark's sister but also for Mark.

He walked in once on Mark using the restroom. "Are you masturbating?"

Mark blinked. "No."

"Do you know what masturbation is? Do you know how to do it?"

Mark lied to him and told him no, thinking he would leave and let him finish his business. Because… privacy?

No such luck.

Instead Ray Ray pulled his penis out. "Jack me off. I'll tell you what you're doing wrong, so you can be a pro at it."

You have got *to be kidding me!*

Mark told him no, flat out. Unfortunately, Ray Ray was having none of that.

"I can see you've got a boner. Come on, let me watch you jack yourself off, and then I'll show you how it's done."

Mark could see he wasn't taking no for an answer. Reluctantly he began to masturbate in front of him. Ray Ray watched him for a bit before stopping him.

"Look, you're doing it all wrong. Let me show you. Let me do it." He reached over, grabbed Mark's penis and started to jerk him off.

Mark was about thirteen years old at the time.

And it didn't stop there.

Ray Ray was always asking Mark to watch him or let him watch Mark. This was nothing new to Mark, who'd been there before; at least Ray Ray wasn't as aggressive as Mr. S, but when Mark said no, Ray Ray tried to make him feel bad, make him feel guilty for not wanting to give each other pleasure.

It was a weird situation. The more Mark gave into him, the more Ray Ray was turned off. The more Mark said no, the more Ray Ray made him feel guilty and the more aroused Ray Ray got. It proved to be an exhausting battle, and some days it was hard for Mark to fight. He was tired and just wanted things to stop. After he stopped fighting him, Ray Ray left him alone. Was Mark wrong? He didn't care. At least it was over—well, with Ray Ray, at any rate.

Yeah, you've guessed it. There were others to take Ray Ray's place.

One of his other adopted brothers, Raymond, was not just an adopted brother but a friend. They used to practice special songs to sing at church together and he was always extra nice to Mark and

John Peterson, another adopted brother. Raymond used to babysit them when he got older, and his mom also used to watch them occasionally when Mark's mom had to go back to work.

Then came the day when Raymond pulled the old 'I'll show you mine if you show me yours' gag on John, and it worked. John whipped out his penis and then Raymond whipped out his. Mark was shocked at what he saw, because, *damn*, they were two of the biggest he had seen at this point.

Not that this episode didn't answer a question in Mark's mind. He already had the feeling that he was gay. Add to that his secret crush on John, and Mark figured this was his opportunity to see if John was interested in him. He told John he would show him only. Raymond got upset and kept saying that they could have a lot of fun together, all three of them.

Mark told Raymond no. Raymond was black, and Mark was scared of black guys to an extent because Mr. S had been black. The only thing that kept rolling through his head was Mr. S's face. Raymond convinced John and Mark that what they were doing was okay if they listened to Christian music while they did it.

Yeah, really.

We need to establish a timeline here, because Mark was eight years old when Raymond started this little three-way circle between himself, Mark and John. Things would happen occasionally but nowhere near as frequent as things with Mr. S. Raymond

abused John and Mark, not just physically but mentally as well.

Why did Mark say nothing? That was simple. He knew that if he said anything about Raymond, he would have to talk about Mr. S and if he did *that*, his family could be in danger. So in his mind he was staying silent to protect his family.

Back to the timeline, because this went on for a while. Like, eight years.

It took that long before Raymond told someone he had a problem. One of the youth leaders went to Mark's parents and they called a meeting. The boys found themselves in a very confusing place. They sat in a room, the three boys, Mark's parents, the head pastor of the church and his wife.

Mark was torn. On the one hand he wanted Raymond's abuse to come to an end, but on the other, he was scared to death. He did *not* want to talk about this, because of where it might lead. So when it came to the crunch and the adults asked them what was going on, the boys told them that they were all doing it willingly and it was just a game that they were playing.

What happened next took Mark completely by surprise.

The head pastor didn't care about them at all. The only thing he kept asking was, "What did you guys do to my grandkids?" He assumed because Mark was best friends with one of his grandsons that Mark was molesting him or doing stuff with him, which

was not the case at all.

When the truth finally sank in, Mark was devastated. The Pastor had no intention of helping them or getting to the bottom line of what was going on, and that was the end of it. Raymond admitted to what they had all been doing but his way of admitting was by trying to push the blame on John and Mark, insisting that they'd pulled him in. That was a lie.

John and Mark had their little secret thing that they had behind everyone's back and when it was just him and Mark together, they would fool around but it was because they both wanted to. When Raymond was involved, it was forced and Mark for one did not want it.

John and Mark continued to mess around. They became very close and while most people considered them 'the best of friends' they were secretly boyfriends. It was like a Romeo and Juliet type of thing because they weren't allowed to be together alone anymore. With everything that had been going on in Mark's life with Mr. S, he felt so safe when he was with John.

It didn't last. John got upset because of what Raymond did, He thought he could keep going with Mark but he didn't like that people knew they had been doing "gay things" so, he started dating Mark's baby sister as a way of getting back at him. Sounds like a crazy tumble weed family love circle, I know. After a few months, he broke her heart, and he ended up moving away and getting some girl pregnant. It

was what felt right for him and Mark had to move on.

After John came Lil B, John's older brother, and another of Mark's adopted brothers.

Now I just sound like a slut, but Lil B was the first person to show real emotion with me. I wasn't moving from one guy to another, I was just confused as hell. Lil B was someone I held close in my heart because he had also been sexually abused, by his uncle.

Lil B was highly addicted to drugs but he had a good heart; he strived to do well in everything he did. He trusted Mark and Mark trusted him. He protected Mark when other kids would mess with him and he stood up for Mark when he couldn't stick up for himself. Mark remembered there was one guy who used to bully him all the time, calling him faggot and telling people he was going to beat Mark up if he ever got him alone. Lil B chased him down the street and told him if he ever heard that he was bullying Mark again, he wouldn't be able to walk.

And then everything changed.

Lil B and Mark went out to Dell Taco one night. Mark had just turned sixteen and gotten his license, so he was able to use the car when it was available. They were hungry, so they went through the drive through and parked up in the parking lot to eat. Once they started talking, they realized they had a lot more in common than they'd thought. But what

happened then was out of the blue.

Lil B started getting an erection.

When he caught Mark looking at it, he said, "If I show you mine, will you show me yours?"

Oh God. Mark's heart started racing because he started to feel things he hadn't felt before. Yes, he'd had a crush on John. He knew that's what it was, but what he was feeling for Lil B was…more.

His heartbeat still pounding, Mark said yes.

Lil B whipped out his penis and then it was Mark's turn. They started making out, jerking each other off, until Lil B came to his senses.

"We can't do this here."

They pulled out of the parking lot and drove to a deserted alley way. Then it was right back to making out. They sucked each other off and made love in the back of the car.

That was the first time Mark had done anything quite that… crazy. It was so intimate and emotional, knowing they both wanted to do it, and the fact that they were feeling the same things made it much more enjoyable than ever before.

They continued to do things together for over a year, driving out to the desert or the alley. They found a few spots that worked for them even after Lil B moved out. Mark thought he was falling in love with Lil B.

Yeah, you already know it's not going to end happily, right?

Lil B worked out that Mark's attachment to him

was far greater than Lil B's attachmer
he decided to cut it off before things v
Occasionally they would find a way t
out, but they ended the sexual behavior ror ....
of the family'—or maybe it was Lil B's inability to
admit he was feeling the same way. After the year or
so of keeping this up, Mark realized something
important.

His 99% feeling that he was gay? There was no
question about. He was a solid 110% certain.

Day Four – More Family Matters

Today MoMo was coming to visit me for lunch.

If anyone knew a thing or two about doctors it was MoMo; she had been pricked and poked by a few in her lifetime.

MoMo is a friend I met through Donald and Brad, although I stole her away from them real quick. She was a blast to be around because she always got jokes flying left and right. Remember when I said I hung out with all the black girls in Phoenix? Well, I might have been in NYC but nothing had changed. MoMo was my black girl—or as they say it these days, *gurl*. We dance together, we gossip and tell jokes, but we can also talk real with each other. I was happy that she was coming in, because I was in need of a good laugh.

My lunch arrived just as MoMo walked in. She wobbled her way across to my side of the room, wearing the only V-neck shirt that would show all of her goods. Lord knows, he gave her a little extra baggage to carry around when he made those things.

And yes, I'm talking about her boobs.

Luckily Mr. Frankford was asleep or he would have had a heart attack from seeing them.

Anyways, back to me.

I took the lid off my lunch and there were those chicken fingers Donald had the previous day. I was in

heaven! I also had French fries and Italian ice, and thanks to Brad I had some cheesecake that he'd snuck in for me the previous day.

After devouring my lunch, MoMo and I had a serious talk about David and me. Our relationship was still fresh but we had already been talking about me moving in with him. MoMo was concerned because we didn't really truly know each other, but hey, love is love, right?

MoMo gave me smooches on the cheek and went on her way. Kelsie walked in as MoMo was walking out, and gave her an odd glance.

"Are you family?" Kelsie asked. We were only allowed to have family visit.

MoMo gazed right back at her, unblinking, and said, "I'm his mother."

The look on Kelsie's face was priceless.

She began to apologize until MoMo stopped her and told her it wasn't the first time anyone had accused her of being in the wrong. It was all part of the territory of being black.

MoMo left, and straight away Kelsie's hundreds of apologies started up. In order to change the subject, I asked her what was wrong with her grandfather, Mr. Frankford.

"He had a bad fall. To be honest, his age is making it hard for him to do things on his own. His health has been on the decline ever since my grandmother passed away. He hasn't taken her death very easily and I think his body has begun to shut

down because she's not there anymore."

"How long were they married?"

"Sixty-three years."

I think that's an incredible achievement in this day and age.

Kelsie had driven all the way down from Maine to help take care of her grandfather after the funeral. She talked about how her family had always viewed funerals as a celebration of the deceased's life but that they'd found it difficult to celebrate the life of one who was so near and dear to them.

That was all it took for my mind to go off on a tangent again. Memories I thought I'd boxed up and put away for good years ago suddenly chose to surface, and I was plunged right back into them as if it were yesterday.

~ 0 ~

It was the summer of 2000 and Mark's father had been really sick, to the point where the doctors had given him only months to live. Mark's great grandmother passed away, and Mark was sent out to Texas to represent the family at the funeral since Mark's father couldn't go. Mark took the trip with Uncle Roger and his wife. Along the way they stopped and got a hotel room because they didn't want to drive straight through from Phoenix to Dallas.

It was early in the morning, the sun not even up yet and Mark was awoken.

What woke him up? That would have been Uncle Roger, perched on the side of the bed, and

touching Mark in inappropriate areas. When he realized Mark was awake, he stopped, got back in bed with his wife, and promptly fell asleep.

Unfortunately, Mark was unable to go back to sleep. He tossed and turned all night, plagued by flashbacks of Mr. S that shot through his mind, and there was nowhere to run, nowhere to hide, no way of dealing with it other than just lying there and coping with the flood of emotions.

The sun was peeking through the curtains and finally everyone was awake. They packed up the car and were soon back on the road to Dallas. Luckily Mark had his own room at his grandparents' house in Texas once they arrived.

Like Kelsie's family, Mark's family celebrated the life of those who passed, but only if they were a born again child of God. They mourned those who had not accepted Jesus into their hearts.

This funeral was a celebration to remember. They sang and danced, cried and laughed. People told stories of all of the good things that Mark's great grandmother had accomplished in her lifetime. They also told stories of some possibly embarrassing moments that had never been shared before. It was like Mark was learning about this woman for the first time.

The whole trip lasted about a week and Uncle Roger avoided Mark until they had to get back in the car and head back to Phoenix. It was like Uncle Roger didn't know what was going on.

Fast forward a year or two after the trip, and Uncle Roger and his wife got into a fight and split up. Uncle Roger ended up moving in with Mark's family for a while after he and his wife got a divorce. He was on a lot of medication, the reasons for which no one was really sure.

Most unfortunate of all, he ended up having to share a room with Mark.

One night, everyone was roused from their slumber by a crash. In Mark's room that was normally obsessively organized, there were things scattered all over the desk and floor. Standing in the middle of it all was Uncle Roger: he was at it again.

A few months after Uncle Roger came to live with us, I woke up to him touching me again. I pushed him, and he fell and hit my desk and knocked a lot of things over. I was sitting up on the top bunk of the bed when all of my family ran in to see what happened. I told them he was sleep-walking and that he'd fallen and knocked things over. He was family and had nowhere to go, and my dad would have put him out on the streets if I told them what really happened. I guess I was trying to protect him, but I am not sure why. Maybe I still had a fear of death, even though we were far away from Mr. S. Maybe I was feeling like everything that had happened to me was my fault. I was afraid of what they would do to me if they knew what I had been through.

Mark wondered why these types of things kept happening to him. He hated himself, even the way he looked. In his worst moments, he didn't want to live. Mark had frequent nightmares and cried himself to sleep most nights. He was so scared that he would pee the bed at night instead of getting up to use the restroom. Mark became so ashamed of himself although he was the victim.

Sometimes when victims have perpetrators that are family members, they shut out the whole family, regardless of who in the family did it. Mark pulled away from his family slowly, although they were so incredibly close. Mark never let his family see him with his shirt off. He was scared, first off that they would see the marks left on his body from the abuse, and secondly that they would see his body and want to do the same things everyone else was doing to him. The mind works in many ways to try to protect you. In Mark's distorted situation, he reasoned that if no one could see him naked, no one would want him.

Mark couldn't always see the marks on his body but he could feel them when the hot water and soap washed over him. The scratches left on his back from trying to pull away or the scrapes on his knees from being forced down to service Mr.S and his manhood. The bruises on his legs and arms from being grabbed and held down. The sting of the hand prints on his ass from being slapped. Some of the marks were typical for a boy his age and could have come from playing on the playground so people

didn't pay much attention to the ones they could see.

I was young and didn't know why people did what they did, although I had my own opinions. People always told me I was handsome, cute, and gorgeous, so I thought that's why I was being abused. As a result I hated how I looked. I figured that if people thought I looked "so good" with my clothes on, then they would only want to see me with them off and abuse me. I know now that my thought processes as a child were wrong; my fears made every little thing seem scary. But I cannot be held at fault for my fears.

I was getting ready to start high school and I started pulling away from my family. I was hurt, and the more I was hurt by other people, the more I would blame myself and to an extent, my family, even when they had no clue what was going on. I continued to lie to them, but why? Mr. S was long gone and their safety was no longer a real viable threat, so what was I lying for? I wasn't protecting myself by not telling the truth—I was only hurting myself more and more.

~ 0 ~

Family is important and it is a sad thing when someone is forced to pull away from those who love them. I thought it was what I had to do to protect myself from being hurt by anyone else. So, instead of leaning on the ones I should have trusted the most, I ran from them.

David was off work and on his way to the hospital to see me. I was ready to see his face. One thing about David and I that I hated, was that we were in an open relationship. We were allowed to pretty much do as we pleased sexually with any one we wanted, as long as at the end of the night we were together. It was a miserable existence at times. I was always afraid he would meet someone else and leave me out in the rain.

Even though I didn't want an open relationship, I agreed it because I liked David a lot. I had friends who had successful open relationships and I didn't want to push away this great guy just because I hadn't tried something before.

Well, David had been off work for about an hour and a half, and he hadn't shown up or contacted me, so of course I expected the worse. I assumed he was hooking up with someone while I lay there stuck in the hospital. David never really admitted to every time he hooked up with someone; the communication and honesty were non-existent most of the time. But I loved him.

David finally showed up—with Chinese food! I had been craving it, how did he know? My earlier thoughts disappeared as if they were never in my mind in the first place.

While we sat there after we finished our dinner, I seized the moment.

"I'd like to read you something I wrote, a

poem." I had only shared this poem once before. I like poetry. It allows me to express myself, my feelings, and allows me to be myself without fear of ridicule.

"A poem? Where did that come from?"

"I was in the first year of college, 2007 to 2008, and the school year was about to end. My friend Calen asked me to go with him to a woman studies on sexuality seminar. It was a free seminar that was meant to express the sexuality, struggle, and life of a woman through poetry."

The speaker asked everyone to take the first 20 minutes and write a poem using "why" statements. He wanted us to question our lives, our struggles and our sexuality using poetry.

My mind began to flash and the words could not be stopped. The words poured out of me from someplace deep within, and I hastily scribbled them down, letting my mind express itself freely.

Day Four - WHY?

WHY? Because you were my best friend's father and you raped me when I was just six years old.
WHY? Because you videotaped me and my friend and took pictures of us naked. Because you held a gun to my head and told me to suck your cock. Because you pulled the trigger on the gun and it wasn't loaded, even though at the time I was ready to die.
WHY? Because I can't walk into an empty room without crying because memories of your nasty face are all over the walls. Because I can't walk home alone without having a fear of being raped or beaten.
WHY? Because I can't sleep at night; I'm scared you will come to my window and pull me out.
WHY? Because I have a fear of being all alone. Because I feel everyone can see that I have had your penis inside of me.
WHY? Because you were supposed to be my uncle and you were supposed to look after me, but you looked a little too closely and you hurt me in ways I have felt before but didn't expect to feel from you. Because we were going to a funeral for your grandmother but on the way we stopped at a hotel so you could take your sadness out on me.
WHY? Because my family took you in and put clothes on your back. Because one of you made me feel special and loved for the first time, and then you

came inside of me, and every moment and every thought of you as my brother flashed before my eyes and left my mind. Because one of you was drunk and took advantage of me while you babysat me for a weekend.

WHY? Because we went to church together since we were in diapers and I thought you were the one for me, but I only liked the thought of you in my life. Because I gave you a promise ring in fear that I would hurt you. Because I never wanted more from you than friendship, but we were forced together just so I can prove everyone wrong—that we are not perfect for each other.

WHY? Because you were my role model and my godfather, but you took advantage of it, and you woke me up by sucking my 15 year old penis.

WHY? Because I thought it was over until you came into my life!

WHY? Because I put my trust in you and you put your penis in me, and you said you loved me, but you only loved the thought of your cock moving slowly in and out of my body.

WHY? Because I gave you a second chance and yet while I was sleeping you kissed me again and touched my cock the day after Christmas in your condo.

WHY? Because I am starting to like the feeling of everything that happened to me during that immature state of my life, now that I'm mature.

WHY? Because you were my first boyfriend, but I was only with you because you treated me like I mattered,

and spoiled me with your money that you earned by escorting for other men, and you lied to me, saying that the money was from the rich parents that you don't have.

WHY? Because you told me I was going to be your boyfriend and I said okay because I was scared of you. Because you were a senior in high school and I was only a freshman. Because your boobs were the first boobs I had ever seen or touched.

WHY? Because I started falling in love with you my sophomore year. We'd talk on the phone every night before we went to bed, talking dirty to each other. Because we would sometimes fall asleep talking to each other, and the next day be so high sprung and want to touch each other, but we were both all talk and no action.

WHY? Because you were one of my best friends in high school.

WHY? Because you only invited me because you were scared I would have sex with your girlfriends, so we jacked each other, off not knowing that I would like every second of it.

WHY? Because you were the first boy I really fell in love with and we kissed, and now we are best friends. Because I love you more than I have ever loved anyone, even though you are over a thousand miles away, and you are in love with your girlfriend.

WHY? Because I'm scared to go to the doctor. Because I'm scared they will find something left in my body by one of the men who abused, raped, and

tortured me.

WHY? Because every day of my life I have thoughts or flashbacks that could only be cured by sexual acts.

WHY? Because I took advantage of your emotions; I was just horny.

WHY? Because I lied to you. Because I thought you were cute and I wanted to be close to you.

WHY? Because we hooked up in your car behind everyone's back and I liked it.

WHY? Because we drove far away, thinking no one would ever find out, and then we made sweet love. Because I knew I liked you but you only wanted it because you were horny, and I was just another guy to you.

WHY? Because you began to fall in love with me as I started pulling away from you.

WHY? Because I lay in bed with you for many nights, knowing you liked me, but I just needed a place to sleep.

WHY? Because the thought of us being together takes me back to my painful childhood, although you were never there for it.

WHY? Because I hide everything I feel from everyone around me. Because every day I want to cry and run away and never come back. Because every moment I am alone, I think of ways to kill you or myself, because you hurt me.

WHY? Because I don't want to live this life any more, but you keep pulling me back in with your sexual innuendos.

Why?

I told David that this poem was important because it was the first time I had ever written my story down on paper that wasn't in my journal.

Of course, reading it to David brought back so many memories, including what happened the day I wrote the poem. It was such an embarrassing moment for me.

The speaker asked everyone to send their poems up to the front without any names on them. He shuffled them around and he pulled out three poems. He said he was going to pick three people to come up and each of them would read one of these poems.

~ 0 ~

Mark's hands got sweaty and he got sick to his stomach, not knowing if his poem would be read. His gut turned over and he ran to the bathroom to throw up.

When Mark returned to the room, he realized with a shock that the girl at the front of the room was reading his poem. He could tell it was his because it was the only one that was more than two pages long. Mark began to shake and flashbacks filled his mind. He couldn't control the tremors that rampaged through him.

Mark's friend Calen ran to get Adeana, an aid worker who Calen knew Mark had been working with. Together they walked Mark out to her office. Adeana knew what was happening. He had talked to

her about the sexual abuse before but she hadn't realized it was this bad. She recommended that Mark start seeing one of the school counselors for the remainder of the semester, and all through the next semester Adeana promised she would get program funding for him to pay for the sessions.

Mark agreed and counseling began. One of the contingencies was that Mark would receive the copy of the poem he wrote, an easy fix since it was one of the three that was pulled.

~ 0 ~

David interrupted to ask me about the counseling. He had gotten his masters in Counseling so he was interested in knowing how I felt about it.

Honestly? I hated it. I told some of my story to the therapist and after four days she started to blame my family—more specifically my parents—for everything I had been through. I was not going to stand for that. My family are some of the most giving, loving and genuine people I know, and I was not going to just sit there and let this woman who knew *nothing* talk down about them.

David could tell he'd hit a soft spot and grabbing my hand, he told me he loved me. Then he held me for the remainder of the night until I fell asleep. It was only about six p.m. I woke up to David lying on the radiator; the nurse must have brought him a pillow and blanket. I think our conversation worried him because I got so heated, so he decided to stay the whole night.

I looked at the clock and it was just after eight. I knew the nurses were going to come in soon to take more blood so I prepared myself. A young man walked in, the first male nurse who'd attended my room the whole time I'd been in the hospital.

He began to take blood and the tattoo on his arm seemed to jump right off his arm and slap me in the face. It was identical to one belonging to a guy I had crushed on in high school. Trust me, I knew. I would stalk his social media and masturbate to his photos. I could pick that tattoo out of anywhere.

Jacob's face flashed in and out of my head. His *penis* flashed in and out of my head. It was like a strobe lite of images and I started feeling dizzy. Maybe they had taken too much blood and I was going crazy.

When the nurse left the room, instantly I grabbed my pen and note pad, and my hands just went to work.

Day Four - High School

During his sophomore year of high school, Mark was invited to a graduation party by Jacob, a guy whom he looked up to a lot. Jacob took Mark under his wing and always stuck up for him if anyone said anything about him that was remotely negative. He gave Mark the nick-name 'Track Star' and secretly he became an important part of Mark's life. The two of them messed around a couple of times, but nothing serious because Jacob had a girl friend at the time.

They met because Mark was the only freshman in the advanced weight lifting class. They would start every class by going out and running a mile on the track. Mark wasn't a distance runner at all, but he still lapped everyone in the class every time, hence the nick name.

Mark got to the graduation party and was one of the first to arrive. Jacob welcomed Mark with open arms and asked if they could mess around before anyone else got there. Mark agreed because he trusted Jacob and they had messed around before.

And Jacob was so sexy to me!

They went back to Jacob's room and began making out. One of Jacob's friends walked in, a friend Mark knew way too well but didn't know was into the same stuff they were. What surprised him

was that the guy stayed.

The three of them began messing around, all of them naked. The next thing Mark knew, three turned into four, four into eight, and then eight became twelve.

That was when Mark felt *really* uncomfortable and way out of his depth.

"Jacob, I want to leave."

Jacob frowned. "Hey, this is my party and I want to celebrate with you."

Mark's heart sank. "Okay, I'll celebrate with you, but have the others leave?"

Jacob waved his hand. "It's okay, really."

It was definitely *not* okay as far as Mark was concerned.

He grabbed his clothes and walked down the hallway. As he was starting to put his clothes back on, two of the guys grabbed him and pulled him back into the room. Just like that, his clothes were off and they held him down while they took turns sucking his penis and making him suck theirs. Mark was in tears, telling them he was not okay with this and he wanted to leave. What made it worse was the whole time this was going on, Jacob kept telling Mark it was okay and he would make sure no one hurt him.

Jacob was semi-protective in the fact that he would not allow all of them to penetrate Mark but only a select few that he 'trusted'. What that amounted to, was only five of them took turns with Mark.

Only. He let five guys fuck Mark. *And this was okay?*

And then things changed a little.

Slowly the tears turned to moans as Mark was unable to prevent himself from becoming aroused. He didn't know what was happening; he just wanted to be alone with Jacob. The way Jacob kissed Mark while his friends took turns with him made Mark feel so safe and yet so terrified at the same time.

Everyone was able to get off, and about forty-five minutes later the house was full of people and the real party had begun. Mark decided to stay only because Jacob convinced him to. Jacob and Mark snuck away throughout the party just so they could kiss, and Jacob could let Mark know that everything was okay.

When Jacob and his girlfriend went into his room, that was Mark's signal to leave, so he grabbed his things and went on his way.

Over the summer Mark saw and talked to a few of the guys from the party, but they all acted as if nothing had happened. They went about their daily lives as if it had been just another day under the sun.

Some of the guys did not graduate that year, and through the rest of my time in high school I would see them in gym class. They were on my athletic teams, and seeing their faces every day only reminded me of that party. Part of me hated them and yet part of me wanted it again, an internal torture

that I couldn't shake.

Mark began to shut himself off. There were fewer and fewer people he trusted, and he felt like he was the only person in the world who was being victimized over and over again by different people. Could they see it on his face? In the clothes he wore? The way he talked? The way he walked? What was it about him that made him an easy target?

Questions I have yet to find an answer to, even now.

~ 0 ~

Let me take a step back again because high school was a huge milestone for me. While it started out rocky with the graduation party, it was also such an amazing time in my life.

I went to school at Centennial High School. In my freshman year I was the shy guy, who didn't talk to anyone unless they talked to me first. I sat in the back of every classroom and worked alone, even on group projects. Every day at school seemed like a pointless day. I was smart and got good grades, but I wasn't going anywhere because I couldn't open up. I couldn't sit down and listen to all of the science and mathematical stuff. It seemed like school was like a conveyor-belt of education that provided a bunch of useless information that you *might*—or might not ever—use in your life. For me, what we go through in our everyday lives was what really educated us to be

ready for the obstacles of life. I felt like my life could teach a lesson to any man, woman, boy, or girl and no matter the age, they could learn something from it. Every day thoughts like this ran through my mind, it caused me to lose concentration, and I started really hating school.

By the end of freshman year I had some amazing friends that I'd met out of nowhere. This kid Dre started a conversation with me, and the next thing I knew, all of his friends were *my* friends too. I had the best friends from elementary school, but we seemed to lose touch a bit during freshman year.

By sophomore year I began to open up a little more. I started to show people the sides of me that no one knew existed. I met some great friends who helped me come out of my shell and I become active on campus. I was involved in the Christian Club on Campus, Fellowship of Christian Athletes, Spanish Club, and of course Track & Field and a whole slew of other things. I was blossoming more as a person, smiling more and finding myself.

The only thing that was weird about the beginning of my sophomore year was that a few people kept calling me Michael. I didn't know who they thought I was. I was in class with one of the best English teachers ever, but when she looked at me and said, "Michael, tell me what this chapter was about," I was confused—until the guy next to me got up and started speaking. She apologized and said she'd meant to say Stephen. So I finally met the guy

everyone was confusing me with. We had a few other classes together as well. He and I became friends— best friends—and we were known as the triplets because Michael had an actual twin sister. It was interesting but it caught on and it worked. When Michael and I were hanging out together, people would ask us all of the time if we were twins or brothers but we didn't see it, just everyone else.

By junior year everyone knew who I was, as I was heavily engaged and active on campus. It was by far my favorite year of high school, because it seemed like thousands of people who were always asking my advice and talking to me and making me feel safe and happy.

My senior year of high school, I was Homecoming King, Student Council Senior Class Secretary, and involved in many different clubs and activities. I was finally the 'big man' on campus. I would not trade my senior year for the world—I had the girl, the car, the friends, and the most amazing track season, but I was living a lie. I did feel like God was finally giving me my life back, but I felt guilty for living a lie. It stressed me out so much that I got injured at the end of track season. I wasn't able to compete at state, I felt like everything in life was piled on me at once and I was beginning to crumple beneath my own feet.

I was not prepared for what was to come next.

I built up all these imaginary walls of protection with all of my activities and clubs and friends, even

the girlfriends. I wasn't prepared to fall again. I wasn't prepared to feel the pain again. Running helped me leave the pain behind and kept the stress and hurt from creeping in. When I was injured, the running was gone, and I was scared.

High school was great and I did my best in everything, but deep down inside I still hated who I was, because I was lying to everyone. I put on the face and I made it work. I remember senior year, we had a day where everyone dressed in costume. My girlfriend and I decided to be a pimp and a ho but I was the ho and she was the pimp. I had on a plaid skirt, red top and a blond wig. I felt comfortable walking in heels and some people asked if I was gay because I played the part really well. I was in my comfort zone, I was me, and I felt great that day. That was the only day in high school where I didn't feel like I was lying to myself.

High school: a place of nerds, jocks, band kids, church kids, Goths, emos, preppies, the normal kids—and me. I felt like I stood alone. A smile on my face every day, joy in my heart every day, but still tormented, full of fear and loneliness.

My high school career was one big fat *lie*.

~ 0 ~

Mark had a friend in high school, Joe. They were very close for many years but they fell apart. Joe was a huge part of Mark's life. Mark's family loved him, all of Mark's friends got along with him, but Joe had some issues he was not willing to address.

Joe was molested when he was younger and Mark always had a curiosity about him, trying to figure him out. Joe talked to Mark about his experience when they were juniors in high school, after Mark confronted him about touching him in his sleep.

Okay, this needs more explanation.

Mark and his best friends from high school began an annual camping trip, their junior year of high school. Some of them had parents who thought they were too young to go on a camping trip alone, so year one, there were three of them—Michael, Joe and Mark. It was an interesting trip. They had a lot of fun but Mark stormed off out of anger because one of the guys was inappropriate. The night before, Joe kept rolling over and putting his arm around Mark to check if he was asleep or not. When Mark finally did fall asleep, it was to Joe touching his penis.

In the same tent, sleeping on the other side of Joe, Michael was awake and heard noises.

"What's going on?"

Now that he'd been discovered, Joe rolled over and stopped. The following day, Michael told Mark that Joe was rolling over and touching him too, but Joe knew that if he touched Michael, he would be going home with a broken arm. Mark was therefore an easier target.

As the trip continued, tensions grew and during their hike Mark got pissed off and stormed back to the lake to sit alone for a while. Joe acted as if nothing

had happened.

Year two, they were seven, all best friends just after their senior year, and the last year they would all spend together before they went off to college. It was fun. They had paintball wars with slingshots, and spent a lot of time at the lake swimming and being men. Good food, good friends, and they were all very attractive, so Mark was in heaven, secretly. Luckily, he knew how to be butch when he needed to be.

Year three, they were down to five. The first year of college took its toll on some of them so attendance was down. It was the last year they would spend with Jeremiah who had passed away that year. *R.I.P.* He was a great guy, full of energy, who kept them all going and on their toes. He was one of those outdoorsy type of guys, which was nice. Mark got to sit back while Jeremiah built the fires and set up most of the camp except for Mark's tent. They just relaxed and enjoyed a five day vacation in the woods. Every year their destination was the same—Knoll Lake, deep in the forest and far enough away to call it a vacation.

Every year they always had some kind of car trouble, except for year three when things went smoothly and was probably one of Mark's favorite years.

Year four, they were down to four. College was really kicking some of their asses. Mark was the only one to attend all four of those trips; all other years, people were swapped out and mixed in. Year four

was nice. It was the coldest year but they did more exploring. They hiked down to a collapsed rail road tunnel that Abe Lincoln's train used to pass through. They hiked down to the General SPG Cabin and took a tour of the small, fragile building made of logs.

Camping wasn't just an annual trip. It was what brought all of them together every year, just a bunch of guys in the wilderness, learning to do things on their own, taking care of themselves. They got to show off the things their fathers had taught them through the years and let their testosterone rule the woods. They hiked, built fires, went fishing, and caught craw fish with their hands (when Mark says 'their' hands, he really does mean 'theirs': no *way* was he touching those things). They went off-roading, and had stake outs to see wild animals at night by the water holes. It was adventure, with no cares in the world, just the opportunity to spend time with real friends.

Back to the story of Joe.

He got very defensive, but Michael was present and had witnessed it happen. Joe told Mark he was sorry and it would never happen again. They remained friends but began to fall away from each other very slowly. A few years later, Mark went home to Arizona to visit. Joe, Michael, Mark and some friends went out for some drinks, then went back to crash at Joe's place as it was too far of a drive to go back to Mark's parents or Michael's house.

Mark slept on the floor and Joe and Michael

shared the bed. Mark woke up a couple times to find Joe touching him. When Joe got up and went to the bathroom, Mark woke up Michael and told him what was going on.

When Joe returned, Mark was lying with his eyes closed. Joe put his penis in Mark's mouth, and Mark rolled over and put his face under the covers. Joe then started rubbing Mark's penis and kissing his neck. Michael sat up to show he was awake. But still it didn't faze Joe. It was at that point that Mark got up and went to the living room to sleep.

After that, Joe acted as if nothing happened and he was innocent. Maybe he had too much to drink but that is never an excuse. Mark stopped talking to him and still to this day has not been able to confront him about it. Joe told Mark he was sorry about the first time and that it would never happen again, but he still did it again, knowing he would get caught.

Mark lost someone he'd thought was a good friend, one he could trust and tell anything to, one who had gone through something similar himself. His friend had been unable to face his sexual abuse and had allowed it to take over his life.

Surviving is an option for everyone; it's about how we *fight* for our survival that separates us from the rest.

~ 0 ~

Writing about high school has made me realize that it has been eight years since I graduated. That's insane! Where has the time gone? What has gotten

me here? The craziest part is that I am still alive. I'm just a few weeks away from turning twenty seven years old. It's been twenty-one years since Mr. S took over my childhood and changed my life. Time has gone but *God*, I am so much better than I was then.

Beyond high school, beyond the sexual abuse, beyond the self-hate, beyond being gay—I am me, I am free and I feel like things are finally going right.

Blessed. I'll call it blessed.

With that, I kissed David goodnight as he prepared to go home. I was exhausted and my emotions were at a low, uncontrolled ebb. Although the pain had begun to ease, I still felt the need to cry. When David left, I lay there in my bed crying, just letting my emotions flow freely from my body. This was me being free.

Free until sleep took over.

Day Five – Gay Dad

I woke up and my pillow was soaked. There was always the possibility that I'd cried myself to sleep. Who knows?

It was still dark outside. I reached over to grab my phone and saw it was three in the morning. This routine was getting very old very fast. My arms were bruised from having so much blood taken.

I kicked my feet over to climb out of bed to use the rest room and suddenly my leg cramped up. I lay on the floor, rubbing out the knot that had formed. Lying in bed for so long was making me feel like the old men I had to share the room with. *Next thing you know, I'll need a hip replacement.*

The knot finally gone, I walked into the restroom to give way to the liquids of the previous day. While washing my hands, I looked closely at my face and noticed the yellow jaundice film that had once covered my eyes was gone. My skin was still so pale, you could see the freckles that typically blended in with my normal tan skin. I looked skinny. I knew I had lost fourteen pounds in the first few days but *damn*, my face looked tiny.

I could hear the nurses down the hallway heading my way for my 4.00a.m. poke session, the first one of every morning. The liver doctor was supposed to come in that afternoon as well, to check

in on my blood work and talk to me about how much longer I would have to stay in that godforsaken place.

Jay was coming by for lunch today to check in on me as well, so it promised to be a decent day.

Jay is the partner to my gay dad.

Don't get your panties in a bunch. He is *not* my sugar daddy.

Yeah, perhaps I *should* explain.

My 'gay dad' is Big B, and at one point he was also my boss. When I first came out I had no one, really. I came out in a very public way and people ran. Family, friends—some treated me like I'd just ended the world.

Except for a select few.

Like Dee. She was a lady who lived in my neighborhood. Her son used to hang out at the house, and he and my little brother were close. Dee would always support us and help out in little ways that meant the world to me.

Dee sent me a message on Facebook, telling me how much she cared about me and that she had a friend that she really wanted to introduce me to.

Yeah, you guessed it. Big B.

I was going to school for Political Science and International Relations. I dreamed of working on Capitol Hill, lobbying members of congress for comprehensive legislation on sexual abuse. I got to live that dream in a way in college when I lobbied for education reform, healthcare reform, and immigration reform.

Big B is the co-founder of a political Public Relations firm. Dee thought Big B was the perfect role model for me, a successful gay man in politics. Big B took me under his wing and I interned for his company and slowly we became family.

Big B was out of town working while I was in the hospital, so Jay was coming on his behalf to see how I was doing.

Knock Knock

Yay! It was finally 4.00a.m. and my blood was ready to be drawn.

I was nervous because this blood work was going to determine how much longer I was going to be in the hospital. Four vials of blood later, I was going back to sleep.

At 6:30a.m. David walked in the room. I could smell his cologne as soon as he walked through the door. I had been in and out of sleep since the nurses took my blood, and David could obviously tell I was tired. He lay down in bed next to me and held me until he had to go into work.

Breakfast arrived just as he was leaving; oatmeal, toast, fruit, and orange juice. I scarfed down my breakfast like it had been days since I had eaten anything, then I got up and walked down the hallway, just to get my legs moving. After that morning's cramp I knew I needed to stretch and get the blood flowing through my body.

As I walked along the hall, I peeked into a few

rooms, just to observe who had been on my floor.

In one room was a little old lady with tubes and wires everywhere, watching re-runs of Wheel of Fortune.

In another room a younger lady was sitting up, slowly eating her breakfast in a very frail and fragile manner.

Two rooms down there was a gentleman who looked like he had been in the military. The haircut and the way he folded his legs when he read the newspaper, and his posture in the chair gave it away. I then noticed the Marine emblem on the hat lying on his bedside table.

In the room on the same side as mine but in the corner was a middle aged black guy. He wore glasses, didn't seem to look sick but I had no clue what had brought him into the hospital.

Then I did a double take. He looked just like my godfather, and those were memories I did *not* want to deal with.

Day Five - The Godfather

Mark's godfather Tony was a mentor, someone he could go to for advice, and someone who was always around and cared enough to be a part of his life. He was generous and gave good advice; he helped Mark care about his finances and gave him helpful tips on budgeting. He was a great person.

Too bad his intentions were anything but great, right?

Tony was one of the few people Mark had ever had in his life who was willing to go out of their way to see him. Lunch, dinner, a movie, bible study, a walk in the park, whatever—he made the effort to be in Mark's life.

When Mark was thirteen years old, he and Tony started doing bible studies together. They started from the beginning and eventually read through the whole bible. Mark learned every book in the bible from beginning to end and was even awarded a trophy by the church for doing so. Reading the bible helped him learn to think more critically and not just read what was on the surface. At the same time it scared him because a lot of what he was reading made him feel like he was a terrible person, like he was doing everything wrong.

As time went on, the bible studies went from being in the park to taking place in Tony's home.

There were other changes too.

At first, Tony and Mark would sit across from each other, but that progressed to sitting next to one another. Tony began to put his hands on Mark's legs and shoulders as if it were nothing. So, so casual.

Mark didn't think it was nothing. When he expressed discomfort, Tony would stop—until the next bible study.

As Mark was a track and field athlete, he had very big, powerful legs. Tony used to tell him all the time how big his legs were. When he would put his hands on Mark's legs, he would squeeze them and his eyes would roll back.

It didn't stop there.

After the church service had ended, he would hug Mark outside to say goodbye, but Tony's ever present erection always made it pretty obvious what he was feeling.

As Mark got older, the touching became more intense and more personal. Every time they hugged, Tony had an erection. He would grab Mark's butt and say "This thing should be illegal."

His 'compliments' were always about the way Mark looked:

"You're so handsome."

"God made you beautiful."

"I've never seen a more gorgeous man."

He would talk about how tight Mark's pants were, and how he loved the way they looked on him because they were so revealing.

What a difference. Away from Mark's godfather, he was always called a faggot for wearing tight jeans. People said he was gay or had no balls because he wore 'women's jeans.'

What people didn't know is that I wear skinny jeans even until this day for my safety. Okay, yes, I think they are comfortable, but that is not *why I wear them. Skinny jeans are harder to take off, which in return helps you in potential sexually abusive situations.*

I wish I'd the luxury of skinny jeans when I was younger. Maybe I would have been spared a few situations.

The moral of the story is to not judge people for what they wear. You have no idea *why they wear it. For some it's fashion and comfort, and for others it's safety. I feel safer when I wear my skinny jeans.*

We all have our safety nets.

Okay, getting down from my soap box...

The whole situation with Mark's godfather would end in heartache.

Tony was also a minister in the church that Mark's family had attended for over fifteen years, and he was also the praise and worship leader. Whenever Mark would go up to the platform to sing, Tony would sit at the back of the platform, just so he could stare at Mark's butt.

Occasionally he would take Mark to lunch or

dinner and they would talk about life, Mark's future goals and dreams, and Tony would give him advice on how to make those goals and dreams come true. The sexual pieces weren't always there. It was as if there were days when Tony exerted self-control—but most days he didn't.

He wasn't always a bad guy. Sometimes things would be very professional between them and not weird at all, but yeah, most of the time they were.

Tony had Mark's parents on his side, being a minister in the church and all. He would call them and ask if he could pick Mark up for bible study or take him to lunch. They thought he was a good role model. And in some ways, he was.

He taught Mark many things, including how to drive a manual car. He pushed him to be very business and financially minded as well, which at some points in Mark's life became very useful knowledge.

Mark was now eighteen. Graduation was over and it was the summer before he left for college. One day he was at Tony's apartment and they were watching a movie, until Mark fell asleep.

He woke up to find Tony kissing his neck. Immediately Mark pushed him away.

"I know you like it," Tony murmured.

Mark was in tears. "You need to take me home, now."

He lunged to his feet but Tony pushed him back on the couch and sat on top of him. "I know you like

it, so why are you fighting it?" His tone changed, becoming more coaxing. "I know you feel what I feel. We can do this any time we want and no one will ever know."

Mark started to panic. "Get off of me, I don't like this. I don't *want* this."

Tony pinned down his arms and started kissing his neck, rubbing his body against Mark's. He took his shirt off and removed Mark's, in spite of Mark struggling.

Oh God. Mark was drowning in a sea of flashbacks. His tears increased to the point where he couldn't see past them. The only thing in his head was Mr. S.

He could hear himself begging Tony to let go of him, but his body was too weak to move, as if he was back in that dungeon all over again. Never mind that he was eighteen, stronger, and bigger—he felt just like that six year old boy again, weak and unable to defend himself.

Then Tony grabbed Mark's penis and started rubbing himself. "We need a little more room here." He climbed off Mark and tried pulling him into his bedroom.

Mark struggled the whole way. "I'm. Not. Going."

Tony ignored him, trying to take off his pants. "For God's sake, will you stop fighting me? This is going to happen."

Mark pulled his phone from his pocket and with

one hand dialed 911. He held it out for Tony to see. "Take me home or I will call the cops *right now*." All he needed to do was hit the call button.

Tony swatted the phone out of his hand and pushed him to the floor. He pulled him into the doorway of his room.

In desperation, Mark yelled out, "I'm going to stand up at church tonight and announce to everyone there what you're doing to me."

Tony froze.

Finally, a pause from this torture.

Mark could almost hear the thoughts in Tony's head as he worked it out.

Tony was always early to church and it had to be getting close to that time. If he wasn't at church on time, people would know something was wrong.

Tony released him, got up, put his clothes on, and they drove to church.

On the way there, Tony told Mark he didn't need to say anything, because Tony was going to turn himself in to the pastor.

When the service was over, Tony pulled the pastor and Mark's dad into the office. Mark waited, amazed that Tony had done what he'd promised.

When Tony came out of the office, he headed straight for Mark. "I told them everything. I even told them that I was stepping down as a minister in the church. You don't need to say anything."

Then Mark's dad brought him into the office. "Did you know Tony had feelings for you?"

Mark sighed. "Yes, but I didn't know this was going to happen."

His dad regarded him for a moment and then nodded. They left it at that.

What happened next surprised the hell out of Mark.

He'd figured that once his dad and the pastor learned what had happened with Tony, something would happen—*what*, he wasn't sure—but nothing changed. Okay, so Tony had stepped down, but what about Mark? Why wasn't Tony in jail for abusing him? Mark began to pull away from his family even more.

He was later to find out Tony didn't tell them anything about the sexual abuse.

He didn't tell them how he'd pinned Mark down, touched him and kissed him.

He didn't tell them about how he'd grabbed Mark's butt when he was still a young child, and how he'd made comments to Mark about his body.

He made Mark pull away from his family. Mark had believed they finally knew that he had been abused. After all of these years, *finally*, they knew. But they did nothing. And that was the worst part. How could Mark tell them about the rest of his life if they didn't care about this one tiny piece of it?

Tony lied to Mark and he lied to Mark's father.

Mark's godfather was a good man with bad intentions and needed a lot of help. Mark just prayed that he didn't hurt anyone else, because everyone

trusted him with their kids. What if by maintaining his silence and not speaking out, it gave Tony the message that it was okay to go and molest or rape someone else? Mark felt as if he was just as much at fault if he didn't speak out, but he didn't know how to go about it.

~ 0 ~

Talk about coincidence.

The pastor of the hospital chapel walked into my room.

He smiled at me, and then the questions started.

"Can I pray with you?"

"Do you know Jesus to be your Lord and Savior?"

"Do you know he can forgive your sins?"

I sat up in my bed. "My father was a minister and I know the Lord well."

He began to ask about where I grew up and which 'denomination' I belonged to. He then proceeded to ask if I belonged to a church there in NYC.

I told him, "I love God and I practice my faith in a way that works best for me. For me, faith isn't going into a building every week with like-minded people—that is called fellowship. My faith is exactly that—mine—and no one can take it away from me. And to be honest, after everything the church has put me through, I'm happy not to be going into a building full of gossip and backstabbing."

His face was a picture of sadness and confusion.

I couldn't help myself.

"Okay, firstly? I'm gay. Secondly, I have been raped and molested my whole life by people who claimed to know God. That doesn't make it easy to just walk into church." I gave him a hard stare. "I can practice my faith *anywhere*, at any time, with anyone. I choose not to practice with those who hurt me the most."

If he'd looked sad before...

As he walked out of my room, he said, "Forgiveness can heal everything in time."

I began to think about what forgiveness is and what it means.

Day Five - Forgiveness

Forgiveness is a word that is demonized by some, praised by others and used frequently in the process of healing from sexual abuse.

To some, forgiveness means admitting that someone else had the ability to overpower you and hurt you in unexplained ways. It means admitting that you are weak.

To some, forgiveness means letting go of the past, and living your life as if nothing had ever happened. The flashbacks and triggers make this hard to accomplish.

To some, forgiveness means confronting or facing those who hurt you, and being able to put your arms around them and tell them you love them.

How many times had I heard "forgive and forget?" Not to mention the constant reminder that I could potentially burn in hell if I wasn't able to complete this task. I believe forgiveness is much easier then forgetting, because my body constantly reminds me of the pain, small minute triggers remind me of the experience, and flashbacks keep the memories with me.

But yes, I can forgive.

To my 'godfather': I have forgiven you for the pain, hurt, and fear you have placed in my heart, for the abuse that you forced me to suffer. I pray that you

have not hurt anyone else and that you get the help you need.

To my 'uncle': I have forgiven you for not being a role model, and for touching me in inappropriate ways. Regardless of whether you were under the influence or not, you caused hurt and fear in my heart towards my whole family, robbing me of the ability to trust. I pray that you have not hurt anyone else and that you get the help you need.

To my 'best friend's father': I have forgiven you for stealing my childhood, robbing me of my innocence, taking away my virginity and my peace of mind, and for causing a life of fear, hurt, pain, confusion, and tears, filled with flashbacks and triggers that still haunt me today. I pray that you have not hurt anyone else and that you get the help you need.

To my 'drug addicted adopted brother': I have forgiven you for forcing lessons of masturbation upon me. It made sleeping at night difficult when you shared my room, but then again, it's not like I was sleeping all that much anyway. You have done a lot of prison time but that hasn't helped you, obviously. You need to see a counselor and work through your issues. I pray you have not hurt anyone else and that you get the help you need.

To my 'adopted brother/baby sitter': I have forgiven you for molesting and raping me for several years, and I thank you for telling someone about what was going on so that we all could start the healing

process. Please continue your healing. I pray that you have not hurt anyone else and that you get the help you need.

To my 'high school role model': I have forgiven you for tricking me into coming to your party so that you and your friends could use me and make me your toy. I looked up to you, and you made me feel so safe and special during a time when I didn't even want to exist, and for that I thank you. I hope that you can get the help you need and I pray you have not hurt anyone else.

To my 'close high school friend': I have forgiven you for touching me in my sleep on multiple occasions, and for lying when I confronted you about it. I hope you work through your experience with sexual abuse. Healing can be difficult, but it is an important part of our survival. I pray that you have not hurt anyone else and that you get the help you need.

To my 'pastor': I have forgiven you for withholding information from the police, when you knew very well that multiple persons in your congregation had been sexually abused. I forgive you for not caring about anyone but yourself and your family, so much so that you would cover up the fact that your granddaughter molested a little girl. I forgive you for being a manipulator, deceiver, and false prophet, thus contradicting the truth that you preach week after week. I pray that God has mercy on your soul because you have the blood of every one of

us on your hands.

To my 'unknown': I have forgiven you for raping me under a bridge, taking the dignity I had worked so hard to regain. To the 'police' who took the report: I forgive you for not filing my report and for not carrying out your duty as a protector. You will probably never see this but I pray that you have not hurt anyone else and that you get the help you need.

To my 'elementary school bully': I have forgiven you for calling me names, and for throwing me in trash cans and dumpsters, and for making me feel like I was worthless and didn't belong. I know the work that you do now and the bullying all makes sense, because we were fighting the same feelings; you controlled yours in different ways than I did. I thank you for apologizing after reading my blog and realizing what you had done. I am so grateful for that. I can tell you have come a long way, and I hope you continue the healing.

Forgiveness is not just about forgiving those who hurt us. We must also forgive ourselves.

I forgive myself for lying about who I am, for withholding information from my family that could possibly have ended my abuse much sooner than it did. I forgive myself for the sexual 'adventures' I put myself through to numb the pain; it wasn't safe and some experiences could have ended so horribly. I forgive myself for all of the suicidal thoughts and attempts to end my own life, which I now realize is worth so much more than that. I may not have known

that before, but I do now, all too well.

Forgetting what all of these people have done is impossible right now in my life. For one thing, I have posted it all publicly on my blog: what is posted on the internet never goes away. It will always be there for all to see. Forgiveness? I've done that and now I can move on with my life, help others find peace and healing, share my story and give hope to those who have lost all hope.

Yes, forgiveness is an essential part of the healing process, but something else is needed too— the time and the support of others.

Thank you to everyone who has supported me in this process. I have come so far since I made my video, and I am blessed to have such amazing people to call family and friends.

~ 0 ~

"HEEEEYYYY GURRRRL!"

I'd know that voice anywhere: Jay had arrived. I always love the way he welcomes me.

I'm sure my delight was written all over my face. "Hey Boo, thanks for coming to see me!"

"Gurl, getting up here was a journey."

Having to take three trains was quite the headache, for sure. Getting from midtown west Manhattan to Westchester was not the easiest thing to do.

Jay hung out for a while and I caught him up on all the medical news so he could update Big B. Being

in the hospital had really brought something home to me: life is much more important than all the battles we go through. Talking to Jay made me realize that I have so many things to do with my life.

This book is one of them.

Not everyone understands life the way I do. Some days I feel like I have been alive for fifty or sixty years because I was forced to grow up so quickly. I am always complimented on how I carry myself, and how mature I am when it come to some things.

They have no idea what I went through to achieve that maturity.

We all have our inner child that loves Saturday morning cartoons, cereal at midnight and rollercoasters. The majority of the time I suppress mine, preferring to remain composed.

I don't get excited by celebrities or artists, I hardly ever remember who is who from what movie or who sang what song. I get excited by the little things in life. Like being visited in the hospital by Jay, who by that point I had only ever met once before.

The fact that he took time out of his day to travel probably an hour to see me for a relatively short time, then another hour to travel home, showed me that I was worth his time, that he cared—or that Big B had made him come to see me. (giggle).

I have always lived by two important mottos of my own creation.

**"Anything and everything in the world can
be changed, if you have the heart and mind to
change it."**

**"Time is precious. Share it with those who
are also willing to share their time with you, and in
that time, take chances, make memories, and
always smile."**

I always seem to find myself in a place where I
wonder about many things. I wonder how I still have
a heart.

Because I wouldn't get far without it?

But seriously… After all the pain and hurt and
torment I've endured, how do I still have the ability to
love, to serve others, to smile? I guess that while a lot
of things were stolen from me, there was one thing
that could never be taken from me—the love I had to
give. And through that love, I found the ability to
smile, and with my smile I found the passion to serve.

I have been in love a few times. I've had my
heart broken a few times. But it's my drive to find
real, true, honest love that keeps my heart beating
every day.

I see that love between Jay and Big B, and it
gives me so much hope that one day I will have that.

Jay stayed until David arrived, then made his
way back down to the city.

David was in a great mood. It was Friday so he

had the next two days off work. I wanted him to go out and have fun, and not worry about me being in the hospital.

Yeah, that wasn't going to happen.

David actually reminded me that the following night I had a huge event that I wouldn't be able to attend since I was stuck in the hospital.

I'd better explain.

A few years back, my mom was diagnosed with breast cancer, and I'd done my bit to raise money to support those who have been affected by it. I had done all the walks, I'd shaved my head, I purchased all of the pink I could find and participated in many of the typical fundraising activities. But that year, I wanted to do something different.

So… I produced, financed, and modeled in a breast cancer awareness calendar called 'Real Men Wear Pink.' The following evening's event was to sell the calendars and raise money, our last big push before people stopped buying calendars for the year—and I was going to miss it. David agreed to go and sell the calendars for me, because he knew how much money I'd put into making this happen.

Dr. Rosenswag came into my room and after four blood tests that day, we finally had some good news. My liver enzyme levels were below 1500, a drop of 4000 from since I was admitted.

This was good news!

Then came the not-so-good news: I was not allowed to leave the hospital until my levels were

below 1000. That meant possibly a few more days in hospital. I was beginning to despair of ever getting out of there.

The nurse walked in to do my 8.00p.m. blood work, and I was ready to eat again. My dinner was kind of small, so I asked David if he would go pick something up for me.

When he returned with a cheese burger and sweet potato fries, I didn't care who saw me give him an enthusiastic kiss. *Thank you, David!*

Happily muzzy in a food coma, I knew sleep wasn't far off, but I wanted to enjoy David's company for a little longer before he left to go home. Once again we watched HGTV and talked about how we wanted our home to look one day. Though our relationship was young and new, we still liked to talk a lot about the future. Maybe we were moving too fast. Sometimes when you go too fast, there's always the danger of burning out or crashing, and it scared me to think that could happen to us.

It had been six months before I'd gotten David to give me the time of day. We met at Six Flags, of all places. He was getting off a ride with his friends, and my friends and I were getting on it: we had one of those speed passes so we were able to go through the exit to enter the ride. Donald and Brad had met David before, and they introduced us. We gave each other That Look—yeah, you know the one—and then we went our separate ways.

I got home to find a friend request from David

waiting on Facebook. I accepted the request and started a conversation. We talked about going on a date, but he was always busy. We discussed the possibility of meeting up to cuddle up and watch movies, but he would always back out. I tried and tried, and then I just gave up.

Remember my motto? Share my time with those who are willing to share theirs? Well, it seems like David wasn't interested in sharing his.

One night I got this long, rambling message about me being the only good guy left in the city, and how he wanted to cook dinner for me. I assumed he was between boys and someone had broken his heart. I figured it was up to me to be the one to fill it. After a few dates, he apparently realized he should have given me a chance sooner.

And here we are today.

My eyes were heavy and I could feel David slip out of bed to head off home, but I was too tired for words. He kissed me on the cheek and left me to my sleep.

I was awakened at 11.p.m. by nurses running and talking loudly: something was clearly wrong. They went around and closed all of the doors in the wing. I got up to peek out of the small window on the door, but could see nothing. They were in and out of the room where the older black man was, the one who reminded me of my godfather. Judging by the way the nurses were frantically rushing around, I guessed he'd passed on.

My godfather...

Damn my messed-up brain.

Once again I was swimming in memories.

Why can I not shake this? Will there ever be a time when I am free of them?

Day Five- The Godfather: Second Chances

Mark had been living in Oregon and was home visiting family. His godfather contacted him and asked if he could take Mark to dinner; he wanted to apologize for what he had done to him.

Mark was happy about this.

"I forgive you and I'm willing to give you one chance to make things right." He went with Tony to dinner and things were fine. After, he took Mark straight home and his apology seemed very sincere. Mark couldn't help feeling that maybe Tony *had* gotten the help he needed, and was finally dealing with his issues.

A few months went by, and Mark was home once again for winter break. Tony took him to lunch. Before Mark got into his car, Tony hugged him.

Well, what do you know? Tony had an erection.

Mark told him it was inappropriate and that Tony shouldn't have hugged him at all. Yet for reasons Mark couldn't fathom, he still went to lunch with him.

During lunch Tony insisted on rubbing Mark's legs.

Mark took a deep breath. "You need to stop, *now*, or I will make a very public scene and have you arrested for sexual harassment." To Mark's relief, he stopped, and everything went back to normal. They

had a good conversation during lunch and then Mark asked Tony to take him home.

Tony parked in front of Mark's house, but before Mark could get out, he locked the car doors.

"Look, there's something I have to tell you before I can let you go."

Mark's first thought was that Tony was going to apologize for earlier.

Yeah. Not even close.

"You're gorgeous and I can't stop thinking about you." Tony locked gazes with him. "I love you and I know we could be so happy together."

Was he for *real*?

Mark kept his cool. "Tony, this is never going to happen. You got that? Now please, unlock the door."

Tony appeared incredulous. "How can you expect me to keep my hands off of you when you look like *this*? You're sexy and that butt of yours is amazing. Those pants were made for you, that's for sure, but they should be illegal because I can't keep my hands off of you."

Oh hell.

Mark's heartbeat sped up. "You *know* that any physical activity or unwanted inappropriate touching is illegal. You need to stop to this."

Tony obviously hadn't heard a word Mark had said. Either that, or he was choosing deliberately not to hear. "You're perfect. We could be perfect together."

Mark had had it. "Let me out now, and *never* talk to me again."

He'd given Tony one last chance to make things right, and Tony had ruined it, unable to control his implosive sexual desires. He was in serious need of help to deal with his issues. Tony was not someone who should ever be around children. Mark knew in that moment that two things needed to happen: Tony needed to be registered as a sexual offender and he needed to go to counseling to get help.

Mark had given him a second chance. Those don't come around often. While he'd forgiven Tony for what he'd done to him, he would never give Tony another opportunity to hurt him.

~ 0 ~

People tell me it was my fault and not his because I wore tight jeans, and showed off things that were never meant to be shown.

Seriously?

I was told that *he* was not the bad guy—*I* was, because I let him do what he was doing. *I* was the bad guy for going with him so many times.

The really sad part? I believed them.

I believed that *I* was the issue, that *I* was the one with the problem. I hated myself, and I begged for God to forgive *me* for seducing *him*. How fucked up was that? How could I have been so *stupid* as to believe that load of crap?

I lay back in my bed. All I could think of was the pastor of the church, and how he had abandoned

me and all the other kids that he knew of in the church that had been abused. I couldn't help but think of how much healing I could have done if that pastor hadn't withheld information from people.

So I decided to write him a letter.

Day Five - Dear Pastor Smith

Before we get to the letter part, I guess there's something I need to do.

As they say on the X-Files, 'the truth is out there', and I've told my truth.

At last.

So maybe it's finally time to stop hiding behind this person who isn't really me. Mark made it easier to tell you about the abuse, but yeah, maybe it's time to let Mark go and be me—Stephen. There's no need to hide anymore.

I mean, I have to face life as myself, right? And this letter was the first step.

So let's talk about my pastor.

I grew up going to a small church in Phoenix. The pastor's daughter was a singer in the church, her husband was the drummer, and his other son-in-law was an usher. The whole family was active in the church, some lived in the church apartment, and some were ministers, singers, and musicians.

My father was the assistant pastor. Our family was also very involved in the church, as teachers, singers, ministers, and musicians. We were in church every Sunday morning, Sunday night, Wednesday night, and Friday night, and sometimes we were there every day of the week.

The pastor was a very jealous man. He didn't

like it when others dressed nicer than him or anyone in his family, or drove a better car. If that happened, he would trade his car in or they would go buy new clothes. They were a money hungry family that didn't really care about the well-being of the congregation. It was always only about them, and if anyone got in the way, they were gossiped about, put down, shut out, or forced to quit the church.

What I remember most about growing up in that church? It was always the elders who were right. We were never allowed to talk back to anyone or contradict them. If we did this, we would get into trouble. The pastor's wife was always putting down my mother and talking a lot of trash behind her back. When it got to the point where I'd had enough, I went straight up to her and told her to keep her mouth shut. The head pastor would always ask my mom why she was so jealous of his daughters, and my mom went home crying after most services. It was not a church that I would ever willingly attend.

I loved going to church in general because I loved the music. That was mainly my dad's domain, and I loved to sing. It always gave me so much hope. But at the end of the day, this church was a place of mandatory attendance that stole from, put down, backstabbed, and lied to its members.

Ministers of other churches were put down from the pulpit. Members who'd left or who were forced to leave, were talked about behind their backs, and

anyone who stood up against the evil of this church was immediately turned into an outcast.

As I've said before, my parents didn't have much, and it was rare for them to get new things. I remember when my dad went to trade in our old, beat down car that sometimes wouldn't even start for a Chrysler 300. The next church service, the pastor's oldest daughter came driving up in a new Dodge Charger to try and one up my family who lived and survived pay check to pay check.

When my father was sick, the pastor and his family would never do anything to help my family stay afloat, but almost every other member in the church did. They brought groceries, helped do our laundry, helped keep our electricity flowing and our water running. The pastor and his family were so stuck in the politics of the church that they apparently felt they were too good to help anyone else.

For the pastor and the pastor's wife's birthdays, we always took up a special offering and passed out birthday giving envelopes to put more money in the pockets of the head of the church, while taking more from the pockets of those who had little.

I can remember when I talked to the head pastor, his wife and my family about the sexual activity that was going on with a couple of us boys. All the pastor could say is, "What did you guys do to my grandkids? Did you subject my grandsons to your homosexual ways?" He could care less about anyone other than his family and himself. We were three boys

who were struggling, abused, full of fear and torment, and he was unwilling to help in any way at all. We were reaching out to find hope and help. What we ended up with were personally dug graves that said one way ticket to hell.

He leads and teaches people of all age, race, gender, sexuality, and economic backgrounds. He has an opportunity to touch people's lives, but instead he leads them away from the church and with an extremely bad taste in their mouth. I can personally list ten or so families that have been affected the same way mine was. It will never stop until his impeachment or letter of resignation is put into place.

You know what? That's a really good idea.

Dear Pastor Smith,

My name is Stephen Land JR. I am sure you remember me because I was very active in your church, Last Revival, throughout my entire childhood. From leading praise and worship to teaching the children in children's church, my activeness had been prevalent. I am writing to you because I have been hurt and abused by members of your church under your leadership. For many years I was in denial about the abuse because my abuser was a friend, mentor, and minister of the church. Minister Tony had a reputation for being good with the young adults and teens in the church, mentoring them and doing private bible studies with them outside of the scheduled church activities. I looked up to him. He

taught me how to drive, treated me to many lunches and dinners that included bible studies, and had me over to his home. In my mind I separated his good deeds from the abuse and I continued my involvement with the church and the private bible studies, despite the abuse.

I was thirteen years old the first time the inappropriate actions began. He was hugging me outside after church. He told me I was handsome and his erection solidified his feelings. He continued to grab my butt and told me that a butt that big should be illegal. His advances continued after every service, every week, and became more and more inappropriate each time. When I was eighteen I was at his home watching "Star Wars" and I fell asleep on his couch. I woke up to him on top of me, rubbing his penis against mine. I told him to get off of me and he refused, holding me down, kissing my neck and telling me over and over again that I do it to myself by wearing pants that were too tight and showed off 'my goods.' Tears rushed down my face as he began performing oral sex on me and told me we deserved each other. He pushed me down, and I told him I would tell everyone, including the police. He stopped immediately and gave an empty apology, saying it would never happen again. Things did slow down and I stopped talking to him, eventually cutting him off completely.

I went off to college, and on my winter vacation I decided to give him a second chance. We went to

lunch, we talked, and things were fine. On the way back to dropping me off at home, he rubbed my leg and told me I will always be his and that I could never run from him. He locked the doors and told me he was not taking me home until I admitted I loved him as much as he loved me. He wanted me to run away with him to San Francisco so we could be together, I refused and pulled out my phone to call my father, I told him I would dial the number if he did not take me home. He took me back to my parents' house and I have not talked to him since.

In October of 2011, at twenty-one years old, I had a break down, suffered flashbacks, attempted suicide, and no one was there to stop me. I had everything set up to kill myself. I looked down at my dog Layla, who sat there staring at me as if she knew what was about to happen. She jumped up and started whining at me, begging me not to do it. I told her to go lie down. Usually she listens but this time she was begging me. Her whining only got louder and turned into a bark, and I stopped. I sat at my kitchen table, opened my computer, turned the web cam on and just talked about my abuse, my sexuality, and my thoughts of suicide. This was my first and only attempt at suicide but I had many thoughts and planned out diagrams of how I could make it happen.

Child sexual abuse is an issue in your church. I am not the only one who has been abused. I have been contacted by at least ten others who have admitted to being abused by someone in your church

and under your leadership. Usher Peterson, Sound Man Pulaski, Minister Tony, Minister Ray Ray, and Attendee Sarah are among the abusers who took advantage of all of us children under your leadership.

I believe there is a passage in the Bible that states that one who harms a child should be cast into the sea with a stone put around his neck. Jesus did not stand for allowing anyone to harm his children. You, sir, have allowed too much harm to come to children under your leadership. The members of your congregation have the right to know that there are perpetrators in their midst. The neighbourhood in which your church sits deserves to know that there are perpetrators at your church. This is an issue of safety and you need to have zero tolerance for this kind of abuse or behaviour in your church, as Christ had zero tolerance for this kind of behaviour.

Stop covering up your sins and the sins of your church, and start taking responsibility for the pain, fear, hurt, anger, and abuse that now haunt all of us who have been abused in your church. I hope that you take this information as seriously as I do. The problem of sexual abuse has been ignored for too long, and unfortunately the church is right in the middle of it all. The short term and long term effects of sexual abuse are infinite and cannot be taken back, but you can start the healing process for those who have been hurt by bringing awareness and seeking out others who may have been abused. As a leader and

the head of your church, you are obligated to bring these things to light.

With respect,
Stephen Land.

My mind was caught up in a tornado of emotions, and once again I fell asleep, my pillow awash with my tears.

Day Six — Letters

I woke up feeling refreshed, just as the nurses were entering my room. The most beautiful thing about these early mornings was being able to watch the colors in the sky as the sun rose to greet the newly blossomed flowers of spring.

Yeah, you can tell that I was in a great mood that morning, although I wasn't quite sure why that should be.

While my blood was being sucked into the vials, all I could think about was the letter I'd written to Pastor Jones. I was determined to send it, although that presented me with a problem.

How could I get this letter into his hands? Could I mail it to the church or send it via e-mail? How could I get the congregation to see the words written on this page?

I decided to post the letter publicly on my Facebook profile and on the church's official Facebook page. That way, *everyone* would get to see it.

Writing this letter had an effect I hadn't foreseen. There were so many people out there who I felt needed to hear from me. They needed to know what I'd been through.

And then it came to me.

I had a few more letters to write—starting with

one to myself.

I'd spent so long living in self-hate and battling with myself to find who I was in this world. I was a drop of color in a world of darkness, but I treated myself like I was a drop of darkness in a world of color. It was time for me to be true to who *I* was. Not the person I *thought* I was, nor the person others had forced me to see myself as.

It was time for some home truths.

~ 0 ~

Dear Self,

You are beautiful the way you are. You are smart, talented, and have a world of experience. You light up a room when you walk in, give the best hugs and make everyone happy.

You tend to put others before yourself, but recently you have realized that you are just as important. You are taking care of yourself for once. Go back to counselling to find a sense of who you are. You are sharing your story to find healing for yourself and to help others find healing for themselves.

You are almost twenty-seven years old and you have accomplished more than most people do in a lifetime. You utilized the bad in life to bring about positive change in the world. You lobby members of congress for the betterment of those who have been hurt by others. You carry yourself with respect and dignity and don't allow anyone to walk all over you.

You show the world that there is a place for

everyone and that everyone deserves love. People look up to you, they love and care about you, not because of what you have been through but because of who you are.

Your heart is on your sleeve. You share your love with anyone who is willing to take it. You give, not to receive but because you care. You are an extraordinary person with charisma, you're fierce, strongly motivated and eager to please.

You are beautiful and deserve to *know* you are beautiful. Your heart is meek and humble. Your smile is honest and hopeful. Your eyes are soft and full of peace. Be yourself. Let your light shine and grace will find you.

No matter how hard life may seem, no matter how difficult the road may be, be *you*. Be true to yourself and never give up on your dream. Your story will heal the world and give hope to the broken, so don't hold onto it but let it go. Give it to those who need it.

With all the love in the world, be the reflection of your future, not of your past.

-Stephen M Land

~ 0 ~

Wow!

The weight that lifts off of you when you are able to say words of inspiration to yourself.

I can't wipe this smile off my face, but I also can't wipe away these tears from my eyes.

All I can do it keep writing.

~ 0 ~

Dear Family,

Mom, Dad, brothers, sisters, grandmas, grandpas, aunts, uncles, cousins—please hear me out.

I am sorry it took me so long to tell you I was hurt as a boy, but I was trying to protect myself and all of you from the same perpetrators that hurt me. I am sorry that I told you the way that I did. I just couldn't face you all, face all the questions, the yelling and the tears. I wouldn't have been able to handle it.

I know we are family, but we fight a lot, more than we should about simple little things that don't even matter. I don't want to fight; I've been fighting long enough. I didn't tell you so you could blame yourselves. It Is Not Your Fault or Mine. It is important for you all to know that I love you all with all of my heart, but you *must* understand.

I am angry, disappointed, confused, and hurt. The signs were there but no one asked. *Why* didn't you ask? I am not sure if I would have told you, but knowing that you cared enough to ask may have been enough for me to talk, but we will never know.

Almost every person that hurt me, the family knew very well. They were members of our family and our church, friends and loved ones. Some of them were always around. I am not sure if anyone noticed when certain people came over that I would disappear after saying my hellos. I am not sure if anyone noticed that I only bit my nails when certain people

were in the same room as me. I would make them bleed to take my mind off of everything else.

Again, I don't blame anyone for what happened to me but I do wonder why no one ever saw the signs. I peed the bed until I was fifteen years old—and no one wondered why? I never took my shirt off in front of the family or anyone until my early twenties—and no one wondered why? I was obsessive compulsive and needed things to be a certain way—and no one wondered why? Whenever the subject came up about moving out of state, I was the first to jump on the band wagon—*and no one wondered why*?

We have had our share of pain, we have had our share of losses, and we have had our share of mistakes. I just want us to grow from here, to move on, to face the facts and to learn from them. We are family, but we sometimes act like mortal enemies; that needs to change.

Last topic; I am gay. You *cannot* pray it away. You *cannot* send me to some camp to try and get rid of it. *This Is Me*. It's who I am, and if you don't like it, then we do not have to maintain communication. I have a strong support network of friends and others that I call family, and if you guys cannot understand, that's okay because *I do*. It is clear as day to me. I have known most of my life but out of fear of losing those who I thought were all I had, I kept it a secret.

I will not parade around acting like I am someone I'm not. If I find a partner, he *will* be with me at family gatherings. We *will* share holidays

together and I expect respect. One bad move, one inappropriate word or conversation is all I need to say my final goodbyes.

I love and respect you all, and I understand that you must stand by what you believe, but we can maintain a mutual respect if you really want to.

It is up to you.

With love,

Your Son, Brother, Nephew, Uncle, Cousin, Grandson,

-Stephen Land

~ 0 ~

Oh God, the relief to write this letter! I know this is the one I feared writing the most, because I know they are not going to like it, but *God*, it feels so good to get it down on paper.

The fear of losing my family is one of my biggest fears.

Yes, I will always be blood, but sometimes that isn't good enough.

Writing these letters is proving addictive. I can't stop them flowing out of me. It's such a cathartic process.

~ 0 ~

Dear Abused, Victims, Survivors,

My name is Stephen Land, and first off, I *know* what you are going through. The days are tough and sometimes the world seems like a lonely place, but *please*, don't give up. I have felt so alone sometimes, and yes, there have been moments when suicide has

felt like the only answer, but thank God, I did not end my own life.

I used to keep three journals. One would be for me to write about my daily life, the things that went through my head, crushes I had, and those types of things. Another was meant to write down all of the bad things; the abuse, the bullying, people who called me names. The last one was meant for me to draw diagrams of how I would kill myself. Plans for how to end my life and take me out of my misery. I only attempted suicide one time, but believe it or not, my dog was the one that stopped me.

I was bullied in elementary school because I got a free lunch at school. I didn't always have the nicest clothes, and a lot of people called me gay. I was thrown in the school dumpsters and people sat on the lid while I fought to catch my breath. I became obsessive compulsive. I carried two or three bottles of hand sanitizer with me everywhere, because I always felt so dirty.

I was sexually abused from age six to age twenty by different offenders, none of whom have faced justice. I felt alone. I couldn't talk about my abuse, I was scared and I pushed away anyone who got close to me. I wouldn't allow anyone to see me without a shirt on. I didn't want to be hurt by anyone else.

I remember telling my mom I didn't want anyone to lust after my body; that was my excuse for not taking my shirt off at the pool. I was an angry

child; I told everyone they were going to hell if they watched certain things on television or listen to certain types of music, talked a certain way, or watched certain movies, I was compensating for the way I felt about myself.

Sometimes my family would rent a movie when our money situation was decent. When we walked into the video store, all of us kids went to find what movies we wanted to watch. I would always sneak away to the gay section, just to sneak a peek at the cover of one of the videos.

I knew I was gay when I was nine years old, but being raised in a conservative Christian family, I was not going to talk about that one to anyone. I lied to myself and tried to pray the gay away before anyone would find out. It took me thirteen years to become comfortable with who I am and proud of the things I have accomplished. But yes, I hated myself during those thirteen years.

I am writing to you, not to just tell you my story but to tell you there is hope and things do get better. I am a walking testimony of what faith, determination, and hope can do. Find your strengths, surround yourself with people who will support you, love you and care about you. Reward yourself every week, just because you deserve it. Being a victim is easy to maintain; being a survivor is hard work but we all can do it.

Don't ever give up on yourself! Love who you are because self-love is the first step to allowing

others to love you, and the first step to allowing you to love someone else.

Be brave, sincerely,

Stephen Land.

~ 0 ~

I know this sounds crazy, but my heart felt so much joy at being able to write these letters.

I hope they help someone.

It's not easy being a survivor or victim, or whatever you want to call it. It's also not easy being a family member of a victim or survivor, because sometimes you don't know how to help. You feel like your hands are tied and you are hopeless.

~ 0 ~

Dear Families of the abused,

My name is Stephen Land, and I am a survivor of sexual abuse and bullying. The world has placed stigmas on me and on your children, nieces, nephews, aunts, uncles, fathers, mothers, and grandparents, because of the abuse they have faced. They say we are weak, that we will abuse others; we are gay or lesbian just because we 'let' the abuse happen.

Please don't be like the rest of the world; we need your love and support. We have faced traumatic events and our minds, bodies, and spirits are struggling to repair themselves. We cannot do this alone.

I can remember the words my father said to me when I came out as a gay man and also came out as a survivor of abuse. "The decision that you make

affects the whole family. We will sit down as a family and discus what you will do."

I don't need anyone's permission to be myself or share my story, and neither do the members of your family.

Abuse is not an easy thing to face or deal with. We will all have triggers that will cause us to have flashbacks or cause us to freak out. Learn what those triggers are so you can help us and not add more hurt to us.

Family is defined as a group consisting of parents and children living together in a household. That is it. If you're not willing to be our family, we will go out and find and make our own. Don't push us away.

What happened was *not our fault.* We did not ask for it, so don't treat us as if we are the culprits, and don't make us feel like we have done something wrong.

All anyone ever wants, what we all aim for in life, is love. Love, support, respect, hope, peace, faith—these are all the things we all want. The list may seem long but it can be easy if we have your support.

Don't call us names—the world does that already.

Don't make us feel like it was our fault—the world blames us already.

Please, please, *please* do not use our pain against us. Healing takes time, and in that time we

need you to be there to pick us up when we fall or to be a shoulder for us to cry on when we feel like we can't do it anymore. Don't push us away—hold us closer than ever, because that's what we need.

Sincerely in peace,
Stephen Land.

~ 0 ~

Words are put down on paper for the purpose of being read. How those words affect those who read them will be different for each person. I just wanted to put my heart on paper because this world need more heart, more love, more peace.

It scares me to think that my pain may keep me from living a 'normal life' because people will be afraid of my baggage. Too afraid to love me because they can't understand what they haven't experienced for themselves.

While my heart this morning is joyful, there remains so much sorrow in it because the world has been so evil. It is hard sometimes to think that it also has the ability to be good.

Day Six – Suicide Diary

My mind was so intent on what I was writing that I didn't even notice David walk into the room. I was proud of what I'd written because it was *me*. I was writing as myself and not as Mark. I didn't have to hide behind this fake name when I wrote these letters, and I knew this to be a huge accomplishment. Only six days in the hospital, and I felt free enough to write without hiding anymore.

David saw my eyes well up with tears, and he ran to grab tissues. He sat beside me on the bed.

"Talk to me, babe. What are you feeling?"

I let out a heartfelt sigh. "I am overwhelmed with happiness because I feel like now I can truly be myself. Even though no one has read what I have written just yet, the fact that I could write it as myself makes me so happy."

David took my hands in his. "Babe, you never have to hide yourself with me, I'm not going anywhere and I'll be here to help you through all of this."

Looking back, I'm not sure if David understood what he was getting himself into by making such free remarks. He hadn't read much of what I'd written either.

It was Saturday, there was no work for David, and he would be there with me all day.

Dr. Rosenswag came in just after the second blood test of the day was released. He had a huge smile on his face, and just the sight of it was enough to send my heartbeat racing. I sat there, David at my side, doing my best to take in everything he told me, but to be honest, I was filled with joy and it was difficult to remember it all.

"Stephen, you must have angels watching over you. I just got your blood results and we are working on your discharge papers."

Tell me he did not just say that.

"Your enzyme levels have dropped below 1000, so we're going to send you home."

Oh, God, he did. He really did.

"Before we complete all of the necessary paperwork, you must understand a few things first."

Yes, yes, get to the part where I sign and get out of here.

"Your enzyme levels are still in a dangerous place and need to be watched."

Oh.

"You will come to my office every three weeks to get bloodwork done over the course of the next six months."

Six months?

"We will be putting you on temporary disability until your enzyme levels get back to normal."

Okay, that didn't sound so good.

"You will have low to no energy, so that means no gym until further notice. You cannot be on your

feet for too long, and you will fall asleep pretty easily so don't get lost on public transit."

And getting worse… No gym? No energy? Work was suddenly looking like a distant prospect.

"All I need is a verbal 'I understand' from you, and I'll issue the paperwork."

There was no hesitation on my part whatsoever. "I understand."

I looked at David, and the joy I had was even more incredible then it was when I had woken up to that beautiful sunrise.

I was going home!

The happiness I felt when the nurse came in with the paperwork reminded me of the weight that was lifted off my shoulders when I came out of the closet.

It was a moment of unspeakable joy that cannot be expressed in words.

The moments that lead up to that joy were hard, and certainly not easy, but that moment of relief was a feeling no drug could give, a feeling no other human can provide, a feeling that you are gifted by God.

And right then I was immersed in the memories of what had led up to that moment.

I remember sitting in Elizabeth's apartment. She was one of my newest best friends. We had talked about her allowing Layla, my dog, to stay with her since Layla wasn't allowed in my apartment. We had slowly let Layla go back and forth between both

places, just until I was brave enough to not have her with me full time.

I walked over to Elizabeth's apartment, and she opened the door with that look on her face. I knew the one. *Oh God, Layla, what have you done now?*

It seemed Layla had started chewing on her baseboards. "Stephen, you need to take her for a few days so we can adjust what she has access to in here."

See, Layla was supposed to be with Elizabeth that night, she wasn't supposed to be with me. And yet if she hadn't been with me, I wouldn't be here now. Layla was my angel who saved me from attempting suicide.

You knew this was coming, right?

It was 2003 when my English teacher told me to start keeping a daily journal. She was always intrigued with the things I would write about. I started turning my journal over to her to read, and she loved my work and loved the way I wrote.

"Your stories are fun and adventurous, but I get the feeling that you're never really putting part of yourself into it; you're just telling a story. You need to write with more feeling."

So I wrote a story about my dad and his health struggles. When she read it, she told me that I should always write with the complex feelings I have, rather than the simple thoughts.

It was 2005 and I was fifteen years old when the nature of my journal changed; it was no longer a daily journal, but a diary where my thoughts and

feelings collided.

This was my suicide diary.

I planned to end my life, but I couldn't decide on how to do it. I would write and draw up diagrams to figure out the best way.

I was in high school, the peak of childhood where the transformation into independence begins. For me, that was complicated because let's face it, I had peaked early. Life had forced me to grow up at an unwilling pace that caused my mind and emotions to go on a journey I was ill prepared for.

The matter-of-fact way I wrote in my diary chills me now.

Jumping in front of a car:

Easy, we live near a road with heavy traffic I could make it look like an accident and no one will ever know that I jumped. Right off of T-Bird Road there are more than enough cars to make this easy. Would anyone actually care if I died? Who would go to my funeral? I have a few amazing friends I know would be there, but who else would go?

I know why that gives me chills. It was like I'd died emotionally, unwilling and unable to feel anything, and all the while I was going through this transformation. I prayed to be able to feel again, the tears rushing down my face to welcome the fear and emptiness I held inside. I screamed in silence, for someone to hear me. With my tears, I poured out my thoughts, writing them in my diary.

I am what I am because they did this to me, I feel nothing because I am numb from the pain my body was forced to become accustomed to.

My life no longer has meaning and the world would be better—I would be better—if I wasn't around.

Would anyone care if I died? Because they don't seem to care that I am alive.

Thoughts flooded my mind and my body began to weaken, as if my thoughts and emotions were forcing me to make a decision on how to take my life.

Hang yourself, it's quick and easy...

But it could take too long and I'd feel the pain...

Jump in front of a car...

But what if I survive? What would I say to people?

Drown yourself...

That could take too long. And where would be easiest? A pool, the bath...

Climb up to the top of a building or something and jump...

At the very least it would break all of my bones and no one would want to hurt me again...

Remember the cartoons, with the little red devil on one shoulder, the angel on the other? That was like the argument going on inside my head. There were *always* voices in my mind. From age fifteen to twenty, I filled out three whole diaries of suicide drawings, planned attempts and words of self-

destruction.

On my twentieth birthday, I burned the journals as an attempt to move on and find some sort of healing. I'd always looked at suicide as a selfish and cowardly attempt to control the uncontrollable.

Yeah. I was such a coward.

A year after burning the journals, I attempted suicide, and failed.

Which brings us to that day…

I sat in my little studio apartment in Oregon and broke down. There were no more words to be written to make sense of it all, no more miles to be run to ease my mind. This was it. I couldn't take any more of the pain, the flashbacks, the guilt… As I got everything ready, tears filled my eyes and trickled down my cheeks.

After all the planning, the diagrams and the endless back and forth inside my head, I'd finally made up my mind how I was going to exit this world.

A hanging. It was the best way.

That didn't mean it was going to be easy.

I stood on the table, a rope around my neck, shaking in terror. Layla stood beside the table, staring at me as she began to whine and bark. Since I'd first acquired her, Layla had been a very calm and quiet dog, but with that sense that dogs seem to possess, she knew what was happening.

I yelled at her. "Go lie down in your bed, girl."

She growled at me and put her paws up on the table, her eyes never leaving me. Then her growls

became barks, so loud they echoed around the small apartment.

Like I could continue with her barking like that. Not to mention the fact that I couldn't look at her, not when she kept staring at me. *Please, girl, don't, okay?* I put up with the noise a little longer, and then I got down from the table with the intention of locking her in the bathroom so I could do this thing. What did Layla do as soon as my feet hit the floor? She jumped on top of me and began to lick my face.

When was the last time I'd been on the receiving end of such unconditional love? Not for a very, very long time.

I removed the rope and sat there on the floor, hugging my dog.

You know the rest.

Most stories like this one don't have a happy ending, but I got lucky. I was given a second chance at life, and I'm using that second chance to tell my story.

I've already told you what happened next. After my failed attempt I sat down at my computer, turned on my web cam and started talking. I opened my mouth, and Stephen Land finally came out.

Before I get into that part, I need to be very honest and open with you.

My whole life, I had been told by family, teachers, friends, and coaches that I was great at everything I did. They told me I had a big heart and could achieve anything I put my mind to. They told

me, "I love you," and that my hugs were magical and made them feel better, even when they felt great already. I was always told that I was handsome and was going to break the hearts of many girls. I was taught skills at a young age that would make me perfect for the workforce as soon as I was of age. Making money was always easy for me because I was an entrepreneur and could sell pretty much anything.

So what was my problem?

I never believed any of it.

Internally I was battling with myself, hating everything about me. I never felt I was good enough and in spite of what people said, I always felt so unattractive. I have a huge family and a lot of friends, and yet I always felt so lonely. Lonely because I had no one to talk to who was facing the same things I was. Lonely because I was taught that I was supposed to be separate from the world, and yet everything I knew was of the world.

Self-hate was something I accepted as a part of my life. I was never going to be what everyone said I was, because no one could see the real me.

Imagine a pre-teen going through puberty, already pumped full of emotions and confusion about the changes happening in his body, and then top that with hatred towards him because of the abuse he suffered, over which he had no control. Imagine a young boy looking at himself in the mirror and crying because he hated what he saw. Imagine a young boy crawling into his parents' room, crying and screaming

in pain in the hope that someone would see past the tears into his hurt and fears.

No one saw the signs. No one could read past the preconditioned thoughts they'd put into their own minds about what I was, because my smiles overshadowed the pain. They *masked* the pain. Everyone else lived in a world where people were happy because they existed, they were alive and breathing, and nothing else mattered. For me, a world of happiness could never exist because I didn't want to be alive and breathing.

What signs am I talking about? Are we talking about tiny signals, so infinitesimal that anyone could be forgiven for failing to see them?

Hell no.

I look back at all the signs I showed that NO ONE noticed or cared enough to talk about. Take a good look. Maybe someone *you* know exhibits the same signs: if so, *do* something. Don't ignore it.

I had problems sleeping.

I became very clingy with my mother.

I withdrew from most people.

And then there were the mood swings.

My temper.

What was bed-wetting, but a sign that I was regressing to more infantile behavior?

My refusal to change out of my clothes in front of others.

My constant anxiety.

The consistent vomiting.

How about the fact that I was researching masturbation, male puberty and porn online at a young age?

Out of the fifteen most common signs of child sexual abuse, I exhibited ten of them, but no one noticed. The inability of people to recognize these signs caused my self-hatred to progress to thoughts of suicide, and ultimately to attempt it. From the age of six to twenty-two, I showed these signs and more. I was slowly dying inside from the stress, pain, fear, and hurt that those sixteen years had wrought on my body. Premature balding began to occur because of the stress, and that didn't help with the image issues I was already having. I was emotionally weak and drained.

Now that I'm twenty-seven, I think back on my life and the things that have brought me happiness and joy, but also the things that have caused pain and fear. You want to know something? I really have lived an amazing life despite the hard times.

At the age of twenty-one I made a video, where I talked about a song by TLC called "UnPretty." It's a song that talks about changing who you are, to make others see you as something that you're not. That was exactly what I had been trying to do my whole life—hide my very existence so no one could see the hurt and pain and the real me. In the video I said, "No one can love you until you love yourself," and "No one can be happy with you until you're happy with yourself."

Those words made me realize that I needed to change for *me*.

I needed to be happy with myself and love who I was, regardless of whether anyone else ever did. I couldn't live my life trying to please everyone else, because I would die before that could ever happen. I couldn't change who I was, simply because people didn't agree with it. and I didn't expect people to change who they are for me.

People assume I am gay because I was raped and sexually misused, I will never be able to change that misconception. What I *can* do is be me; honest, open, and upfront about who I am. I can allow people to see that I am the same person I have always been; I am just being more open and honest with everyone about it now.

I cannot change the past and I cannot predict the future, but here and now this is me and I am finally happy with who I am. For the first time I can honestly say that I love myself. I can look in the mirror and smile, something I had not been able to do most of my life.

I pray every day for God to show me more of myself and to give me peace. I don't have suicidal thoughts anymore. I am happy and that for me is a huge step forward.

Day Six – Coming Out

You already know about the video, the one where I came out, which was subsequently posted online. I talked for an hour, letting it all out.

Well, what follows is some of the things I said in that video, in the order I said them. It's by no means a coherent flow—my thoughts were all over the place—but is simply an outpouring of thoughts, fears, and realizations and most importantly, the secrets I had kept to myself for so long. So forgive me if it comes across as rambling. Please remember what led up to it in the first place.

~ 0 ~

Hey everybody, my name is Stephen Land. This message is for all of my family and friends.

Since I was thirteen years old I have been writing a book. I talk about things that I have been through and how these things have affected me.

When I was six years old, I was raped for the first time. I was raped by this person for about three years.

I got to the point where I wouldn't take my shirt off in front of people, because I was afraid they would do the same thing to me that other people did.

One of my family members lived with us and he was touching me while I was sleeping.

Tears rushed down my face as I revealed things of my past and told the world all of the burdens that I carried. I had no regrets about giving up the weight I had carried alone for so long.

I didn't want to tell my family the stuff that was going on because I didn't want them to deal with my issues, on top of figuring out how we were going to survive with my dad being sick.

My godfather molested me. I didn't know how to fight back because I never had to fight back before.

I was living everyday scared that someone was going to hurt me.

I started going to counselling three times a week in college.

I started blaming my parents and I no longer wanted to go home.

I stopped going to counselling and I got really sick.

I lost sixteen pounds in a few days and the doctors thought I had leukaemia.

I dropped out of school and went home.

Tears flowed from my face, snot dripping from my nose, as I poured out my heart. I had lived a life that no one should have ever had to live, be they woman, man, child—no one.

I started getting better and went back to school. I went to Oregon, where I am now.

Three months after being here, I was walking to the store and someone stopped me and asked me for directions, and another guy came up behind me and pulled me under the bridge. They raped me. I called Paul, my boyfriend at the time.

Through all of this I struggled to figure out who I am, and why all of these things kept happening to me.

I was engaged to a girl.

I told my stories of love and friendship, and I let my pains and sorrows go so I didn't have to carry them alone. I told secrets that I've never told anyone. I allowed people to really see into my heart.

We were going to make our engagement official in February of 2007. She passed away in January 2007.

When I was twelve years old, I started hanging out with gay guys. I was curious to see if that was who I was.

I was taught that it was bad to be gay and I was going to hell.

I prayed that God would kill me if I turned out to be gay.

I had my first boyfriend when I was thirteen.

Slowly, one by one, my secrets were revealed, the weight was lifted from me, my tears kept flowing and still the words kept coming.

I went to Australia and I fell in love. I learned to trust, and we dated for over three years.

Track and Field allowed me to run, and leave my past behind me.

I'm scared to be alone.

Running helped me forget about my troubles and focus on getting to the end. I needed to cross the finish line so the pain would go away.

I became the student body president.

I hate who I am, because I know my family isn't going to accept it, I know the world doesn't accept it.

I know people are going to blame the things that I have been through, on me being this way.

I didn't choose this life for me.

All I want to do is make people love.

People assume men don't get raped. They assume that if men are raped, it's because they are gay.

I went to a conference called Leadershape.

Leadershape is a conference that not only teaches leadership development skills, it also helps students think about their long-term goals and create short term goals to meet that goal. In order for us to truly set ourselves up for the future, we must face our past.

It was in 2010 when I had the opportunity to attend the Leadershape conference.

During my time there, one of the directors had

us all sitting in a circle. She asked that someone tell the group something they have never told anyone before. It felt like an hour had passed and no one had said anything. My heart started beating faster and faster, to the point where I felt if I didn't say something, I was going to throw up.

I raised my hand and simply said, "I am a survivor of sexual abuse." I felt so relieved, like a weight had been lifted off my shoulders. We all continued to sit there for a few more minutes. The director spoke again. While she was thanking me for speaking up, someone else raised their hand. He stood up and said words that I will never forget.

"I have never told anyone what I am about to say, and I never thought I would have the strength to say this out loud, but thanks to Stephen's strength, I can. I am a survivor as well."

The director clearly felt the emotion in the room, and we took a very long break so that everyone could write, think about and talk about what motivates their future.

I talked with maybe twelve people about what I had gone through, and during our small group conversations I had four others tell me they were a survivor as well. We shared our stories and found strength through one another's pain. That was the moment I realized that sharing my story could help so many people, and that I needed to share it in a more significant way. I wrestled with the notion of sharing my story without coming out. Maybe coming out

would give this story *more* significance. I battled with this question for over a year before I finally made the decision to come out and share my story of abuse.

The Leadershape conference has helped me in so many ways. I was able to renew my strength and find my true passions. Anyone who has the opportunity to attend Leadershape should take that opportunity and make the most of it, because it can truly change your life.

Back to the video…

People assume this life—being gay—is a choice.

I smile every single day that I can wake up, breathe, and not have to deal with the pain. I smile so I can make someone else smile, even if my day is the worst in the world.

I tell people that you can't be truly happy until you're happy with yourself. *No one* in the world can make you happy until you're happy with yourself.

I tried so hard to find love, because I wanted someone to love me and not hurt me for once.

I realized no one could love me until I truly loved who I am.

I want people to know that no matter what happens in your life, no matter what you go through, no matter how hard life gets, things *do get better*.

There is always someone who can benefit from your story.

It's not about pride or letting people feel bad for

you. I don't *want* people to feel bad for me. I want people to be happy because *I* am happy.

Life isn't easy.

I always told myself I wasn't going to have sex until I was married, but that plan was ruined when I was six years old.

I thought God hated me.

I wouldn't love so hard if any of this didn't happen.

I don't think God would have let any of this happen, making me this way, if he didn't love me.

I am not going to change who I am for anyone. I'm not going to compromise my life because someone doesn't agree with it.

I feel like I can do great things and I can touch so many people's lives with my love and my story.

I love God with all my heart. I thank God for everything he has ever done for me.

I don't ask God to give me things, or make ways for me. I want to fight for the things I get for myself. I don't want things handed to me, I want to work for them.

No matter what you think or feel about me, I will love you regardless.

I hope people can see that just as God loves everyone, so they should also love everyone.

Love is the greatest gift of all, and without love there is nothing.

You don't have to agree with everything that person does, but you must love.

I have faith that in the end, things will work out the way they are supposed to, and the life that I lived will not go unheard of.

I will not stop sharing my story and I will not stop being who I am.

This is only a piece of who I am. Everything else you know about me is the same; the way I love: my laughter: my smile: my hopes: my dreams: my dignity: my courage: my love for people: my ability to walk into a room and share the warmth of my heart with everyone: my ability to make someone's day turn around with just a smile: me being a clean freak who loves to cook and clean…

I am the same person. You just know now one more aspect of who I am. I hope you can take that and love that piece just as much as you love the rest of me.

~ 0 ~

That cold winter night, I filmed myself as tears flowed down my face. An hour long video confessing all that was held in my heart, releasing the pain I had kept within me for so long.

I experienced that same relief, walking out of that hospital. No more pain.

I came out of the closet as a gay man.

I came out of the closet as a survivor.

I came out of the closet as me, my true self.

No more hiding.

No more lies.

No more secrets.

I am Stephen.
I am gay.
I am a survivor.
This is my story.

About the authors

Stephen Mark Land Jr was born and raised in the greater Phoenix area in Arizona. His family, a very conservative and religious family, was very involved in church activities & events, and all held positions within the church.

Stephen being a young gay man had to make decisions for himself when coming to terms with his sexuality and facing his childhood abuse. He was afraid of being chastised, condemned, and worst of all disowned by his family; he kept the secret of his abuse and his identity as a way to protect himself from being pushed away. At least the love he did have from his family was true and why ruin the only good thing you have?

Stephen has faced violence and sexual violence in many different forms from rape, molestation, verbal harassment and bullying, his story is important and far too common and overlooked. Stephen decided to speak out against sexual violence and bullying after a failed attempt at suicide.

Stephen went to college at both Northern Arizona University and Southern Oregon University where he was highly involved in leadership rolls, student activities, and student life. He studied Political Science and International relations; his love for politics led him to lobby on issues like Student Aid Reform, Education Reform, Health Care Reform, Immigration Reform, More Comprehensive Legislation regarding Sexual Abuse and Bullying, International Affairs Issues and many more. He had goals of running for office but his story became his main priority and now he wants to travel to elementary, middle and high schools, colleges and universities and conferences to tell his story and motivate others to speak out against the violence.

The Race is his story and an important one.

K.C. Wells is a writer of gay fiction and gay romance, who is helping a dear friend bring his story to the world.

Made in the USA
Columbia, SC
24 September 2018